Meet the Shih Tzu

- The Shih Tzu is classified by the American Kennel Club as a member of the Toy Group.

- The Shih Tzu is one of the elegant dogs from China, cherished by royals there for over a thousand years.

- The word *Shih Tzu* means "lion" in Chinese. Shih Tzu, with their mane and proud carriage, were prized for resembling the sacred lion.

- Shih Tzu also have the nickname "Chrysanthemum Face." The hair on their faces grows out in a circular direction, making the faces look like flowers.

- Shih Tzu have always been prized as companions.

- Shih Tzu are alert, arrogant and affectionate. They love people and other dogs, big and small. Everyone is this breed's friend.

- The Shih Tzu's long, flowing double coat makes for high-maintenance grooming and must be brushed every day.

- The Shih Tzu is basically a healthy breed with few medical problems.

- A brisk walk around the block is all the exercise the Shih Tzu needs.

- The Shih Tzu comes in an array of colors including gold and white, red and white, black and white, silver and white, brindle and white, solid gold or silver with a black mask and solid black.

Consulting Editor
IAN DUNBAR PH.D., MRCVS

Featuring Photographs by
JEANNIE AND BANE HARRISON

An Imprint of Macmillan General Reference USA
A Pearson Education Macmillan Company
1633 Broadway
New York, NY 10019-6785

Macmillan Publishing books may be purchased for
business or sales promotional use. For information
please write: Special Markets Department,
Macmillan Publishing USA, 1633 Broadway,
New York, NY 10019-6785.

Library of Congress Cataloging-in-Publication
Data
        The essential shih tzu / featuring
photographs by Jeannie and Bane Harrison.
        p.   cm.
    Includes bibliographical references (p. 87–90)
and index.
    ISBN 1-58245-077-3
    1. Shih tzu.   I. Howell Book House.
SF429.S64E87   1999   99-11045
636.76—dc21   CIP

Manufactured in the United States of America
10 9 8 7 6 5 4 3 2 1

Series Director: Michele Matrisciani
Production Team: Tammy Ahrens, Carrie Allen,
    Terri Sheehan
Book Design: Paul Costello

ARE YOU READY?!

☐ Have you prepared your home and your family for your new pet?

☐ Have you gotten the proper supplies you'll need to care for your dog?

☐ Have you found a veterinarian that you (and your dog) are comfortable with?

☐ Have you thought about how you want your dog to behave?

☐ Have you arranged your schedule to accommodate your dog's needs for exercise and attention?

No matter what stage you're at with your dog—still thinking about getting one, or he's already part of the family—this Essential guide will provide you with the practical information you need to understand and care for your canine companion. Of course you're ready—you have this book!

THE ESSENTIAL

Shih Tzu

The Shih Tzu's Senses

SIGHT

The world is a much bigger place when seen through the eyes of the Shih Tzu. But aside from their view, Shih Tzu, like all dogs, can detect movement at a greater distance than we can, while they can't see as well up close. They can also see better in less light, but can't distinguish many colors.

SOUND

Shih Tzu can hear about four times better than we can, and they can hear high-pitched sounds especially well.

TASTE

Shih Tzu have fewer taste buds than we do, so they're likelier to try anything—and usually do, which is why it's important for their owners to monitor their food intake. Dogs are omnivorous, which means they eat meat as well as vegetables.

TOUCH

Shih Tzu are social animals and love to be petted, groomed and played with.

SMELL

A Shih Tzu's nose is his greatest sensory organ. A dog's sense of smell is so great he can follow a trail that's weeks old and detect odors diluted to one-millionth the concentration we'd need to notice them.

CHAPTER ONE

Getting to Know the Shih Tzu

For hundreds of years, Shih Tzu have been bred to serve as human companions, and their temperaments reflect this fact. In prerevolutionary China, it was a status symbol to own a dog that performed no utilitarian function such as hunting or guarding. The Shih Tzu were highly prized in the imperial court, where they lived lives of luxury.

ALL-AROUND DOGS

Shih Tzu tend to get along well with strangers, children and other dogs, and their small size makes them ideal for today's confined quarters. They are not "yappy" dogs. A Shih Tzu would probably bark if a burglar was picking the lock of your front door. Once the intruder was inside your home, however, your pet would be likely to give the intruder a guided tour! But if you want a small but sturdy, affectionate and appealing companion to share your life, a Shih Tzu fits the bill.

These women are introducing their adult Shih Tzu to a new pup, which is easy to do because Shih Tzu get along famously with whomever they come in contact.

voice. Shih Tzu often like to watch television—and have definite likes and dislikes while doing so.

SELF-SUFFICIENT AND PLAYFUL

Shih Tzu are very self-sufficient. If you are busy, they can and do amuse themselves for long periods of time, throwing and catching their own toys, racing around the house like furry dervishes or curling up at your feet simply for the pleasure of being near. Shih Tzu left alone during the day will usually sleep or play with their toys or perch at a window to watch the world go by. They are so easy to live with that many people with one Shih Tzu eventually get another. Breeders frequently joke that Shih Tzu are like potato chips—you can't have just one. Do remember, however, that the fact that Shih Tzu are not demanding dogs does not mean that they thrive in the absence of human companionship. They are definitely "people" dogs.

Perhaps because of their long and intimate association with people, Shih Tzu seem almost human. Their faces can be very expressive. At times, when a Shih Tzu is watching people talk, you would swear from his expressions that he understands what is being said. Many a squabble has been prevented by a Shih Tzu pawing in distress at the leg of a person who is raising his or her

Even when your Shih Tzu is amusing himself, he will generally do so in ways that get your attention. Your pet might, for example, race back and forth from toy box to living

Even as a pup, this Shih Tzu can occupy and entertain himself.

room until every toy rests in a pile at your feet.

HAIRY FELLOWS

Shih Tzu are one of the few breeds that have hair (like humans) instead of fur. This means that many people who are allergic to fur are not allergic to Shih Tzu. It also means that Shih Tzu do not shed seasonally. Instead, they shed in small amounts all of the time, just as you do. Much of this dead hair remains on the dog and causes tangling or matting. Because of the dog's profuse coat, the Shih Tzu requires regular grooming.

Giving cuddles and kisses to a Shih Tzu is easy—even for allergy sufferers!

THE CHARACTERISTICS OF THE SHIH TZU

Small, but sturdy

Not yappy

Profuse coat (needs regular grooming)

Loving

Affectionate

Great companions

Self-sufficient

Enthusiastic

Charming

Easy to travel with

4

This energetic Shih Tzu is a perfect companion for this active owner.

HOUSEBREAKING CONCERNS

Confine your puppy to prevent mistakes. Regularly (at least once an hour) take your puppy to his doggy toilet and reward him for using it. When away from home, confine your puppy to a puppy-proofed area which has a bed, water, toys and a doggy toilet. The whole idea is not to give your puppy enough freedom to develop bad habits. One day, after you have praised your pet for eliminating in the proper place for the umpteenth time, a light will dawn, and your puppy will understand what you want him to do. I had one dog that came running out for praise every time he used the paper for his entire life once this lesson was learned.

SETTING LIMITS

Given an inch, your Shih Tzu will take a mile. This means you need to think about what you do and don't want your dog to do early on. Do you want to allow the dog on the furniture? Will he be allowed to sleep on your bed? Will he be confined (necessary for a puppy) when you are not at home? Clearly, he is not allowed to run out the front door when you open it or leave the backyard or chew the furniture or urinate on the Oriental rug! Once you have determined the limits, be consistent. You will find that Shih Tzu are very anxious to please, but they need to be taught what you would like them to do.

TRAINING TACTICS

Remember common sense is the best tactic. If the dog removes the *TV Guide* from the coffee table and chews on it every time you go for your morning walk—meaning that you can never catch him in the act—why not just put the magazine in an inaccessible place for a few weeks until he forgets his fascination with that particular object?

Common sense is the real key here. If you get up when your Shih Tzu begins sneezing at you, your pet will, of course, continue to do so. If he is teething on your antique furniture when you are away, why are you giving him this much freedom and where are his chewtoys? The "dominant down" used by some obedience trainers to establish that the owner is "top dog" does not work well for most Shih Tzu. You are already

much bigger than your Shih Tzu and the source of the companionship and praise he craves. Shih Tzu perform obedience exercises well because they want to please you and because you have made it clear what behavior will elicit your praise, not because they have been cowed into submission.

Training your Shih Tzu may be a challenge if you're a sucker for a face like this!

DON'T BE A SUCKER FOR YOUR SHIH TZU

The unique charm that characterizes the Shih Tzu makes the dog

5

Rest assured, your Shih Tzu will love you just as much if you teach him to be well behaved.

tail wagging, many kisses and lots of "Who, me?" looks of injured innocence. The general response when you try to discipline a Shih Tzu is, "How could you possibly be angry with me when I'm *so* charming?"

It's hard to remain upset with a Shih Tzu you've requested to lie down when the dog enthusiastically flips over onto his back and waves all four feet in the air, wags his entire body and kisses the air. And how can you put up a topknot on a dog who is trying to kiss your nose while you are doing it? You have to steel yourself to avoid succumbing to that charm and letting your dog train you, rather than the other way around.

a delight to live with—and also, as you can see, poses an obstacle to training. Training a Shih Tzu can be both an amusing and a frustrating experience. "Bad dog" generally elicits much

CHAPTER TWO

Homecoming

The optimal time to bring your Shih Tzu puppy home is when she is 8 weeks old. By this age, your Shih Tzu pup has had time to receive an additional set of inoculations to protect against disease and, most important, plenty of time to socialize with her mother and littermates. This crucial socialization time provides the fundamentals in teaching a Shih Tzu puppy how to relate to humans and to the outside world, which, in turn, produces a more outgoing, less aggressive pet.

PREPARING FOR YOUR PUPPY

Before your puppy arrives, make sure you have everything she will need in her new home and have created a secure and safe place where she can spend most of her time until housebroken and used to her new lifestyle. Remember, she is still a baby, and it is your job to safeguard her from harm!

It is hard to stand in the way of a curious Shih Tzu; however, locking cabinets is one way to make your house safer for your pet.

8

PUPPY PROOFING

Be proactive when preparing for your Shih Tzu puppy's homecoming by puppy-proofing your home. The best way to do this is to think like a puppy. What would you want to get your paws and jaws on if your were exploring a new human world for the first time? Be sure there are no electrical cords, plants, hazardous household products or other items your puppy might ingest or injure herself with—remember, all puppies love to put anything they can into their mouths. Provide your puppy with toys for this purpose. Shih Tzu of all ages

This Shih Tzu pup is pooped after playing with all of her toys!

love plush and lambswool and yarn and soft latex squeaky toys. They also enjoy hard rubber chew toys, particularly when they are cutting their teeth. Rawhide is not recommended because it softens and sticks to the moustache when it is chewed and could choke a puppy who eats it.

If your puppy tries to chew on the corners of wooden cabinets or other items you cannot remove from the room, spray them with Bitter Apple or another nontoxic but bitter-tasting substance.

YOUR PUPPY'S BED AND CRATE

Young puppies need a lot of sleep. They tend to play very hard and then collapse in exhaustion. A toy-sized enclosed crate (which is also approved for airline travel) with a towel in the bottom makes an ideal bed and den for your Shih Tzu puppy. It is small enough for her not to want to soil her sleeping quarters, so long as you take her to her doggy toilet at least once an hour. Later, you can use it when traveling with your pet. (If your dog is accustomed to her crate at home, you can take her with you anywhere.) If you are using the crate as a bed in a puppy-proofed room or

PUPPY ESSENTIALS

To prepare yourself and your family for your puppy's homecoming, and to be sure your pup has what she needs, you should obtain the following:

Food and Water Bowls: One for each. We recommend stainless steel or heavy crockery—something solid but easy to clean.

Bed and/or Crate Pad: Something soft, washable and big enough for your soon-to-be-adult dog.

Crate: Make housetraining easier and provide a safe, secure den for your dog with a crate—it only looks like a cage to you!

Toys: As much fun to buy as they are for your pup to play with. Don't overwhelm your puppy with too many toys, though, especially the first few days she's home. And be sure to include something hollow you can stuff with goodies, like a Kong.

I.D. Tag: Inscribed with your name and phone number.

Collar: An adjustable buckle collar is best. Remember, your pup's going to grow fast!

Leash: Style is nice, but durability and your comfort while holding it count, too. You can't go wrong with leather for most dogs.

Grooming Supplies: The proper brushes, special shampoo, toenail clippers, a toothbrush and doggy toothpaste.

9

Your Shih Tzu enjoys having a sanctum she can call her own.

exercise pen, remove the crate door or fasten it open so your puppy is free to go in and out of her den as she pleases.

Once your puppy can sleep through the night without having to eliminate, you may want to have her sleep in her crate in the bedroom with the crate door closed. You want the crate to become a safe haven. You can initially encourage your puppy to enter the crate with treats and toys; you may even want to feed her her meals there.

Many older Shih Tzu continue to sleep in their crates. Others like the beanbag beds filled with cedar shavings, which are said to repel fleas, or the PVC piping and fabric hammock-type beds. Any such bed should have a washable cover for flea control.

To help your puppy sleep quietly at night, provide a night light. You may also want to play a radio softly for the first few nights.

KEEPING TO A SCHEDULE

Until your puppy is totally paper-trained or housebroken, adjust your schedule to hers. She should spend the night in her room or pen and be put there when you go out or when you cannot keep an eye on her. The whole secret of successful training is to avoid giving your puppy a chance to have accidents on the rug or to chew on the furniture, thereby developing bad habits. Instead, praise her profusely when she uses the paper or eliminates outside or spends the night quietly in her room.

SOCIALIZING YOUR PUPPY

Once your puppy has become accustomed to her new home and had her final puppy shots, it is time to introduce her to the world. Many people take their puppies to "puppy training classes" so the puppies can learn how to behave with other people and other dogs. If you have no children, your puppy can be introduced to youngsters by taking her to the playground or to a local mall. As she is introduced to new dogs and people and objects, be sure that your own attitude is confident, so your puppy will know there is no reason for her to be afraid.

When investigating new situations, your puppy should be praised and rewarded. Trying to force a puppy

IDENTIFY YOUR DOG

It is a terrible thing to think about, but your dog could somehow, someday, get lost or stolen. For safety's sake, every dog should wear a buckle collar with an identification tag. A tag is the first thing a stranger will look for on a lost dog. Inscribe the tag with your dog's name and your name and phone number.

There are two ways to permanently identify your dog. The first is a tattoo, placed on the inside of your dog's thigh. The tattoo should be your social security number or your dog's AKC registration number. The second is a microchip, a rice-sized pellet that is inserted under the dog's skin at the base of the neck, between the shoulder blades. When a scanner is passed over the dog, it will beep, notifying the person that the dog has a chip. The scanner will then show a code, identifying the dog.

11

Praising your puppy when she does something good will promote good behavior in your Shih Tzu.

Socializing your Shih Tzu with different people and animals will make her more outgoing and well-adjusted.

This Shih Tzu pup eats and drinks from bowls made of metal, which are believed to be the most sterile type and easiest to clean.

to approach something that makes her fearful or picking her up and fussing over her when she is nervous generally reinforces fearful behavior. Instead, gently encourage your puppy to investigate. (Food is a wonderful motivator.) If the puppy is still reluctant, try again another day.

FOOD AND WATER BOWLS

You will also need a metal, weighted plastic or ceramic food bowl heavy enough not to be tipped over and shallow enough for your puppy to easily reach her food.

Your breeder will tell you the food your new companion is used to. It is never a good idea to change food abruptly because this can upset a puppy's stomach. Fresh water should be readily available. Many Shih Tzu owners prefer to use one of the water bottles made for rabbits, available in pet stores, rather than a water bowl. This keeps your puppy's face clean and dry and prevents her from taking a bath in her water dish. These bottles can be fastened to an exercise pen, screwed to a kitchen cabinet or placed in a freestanding holder.

LEASH AND COLLAR

Your puppy will need a close-fitting nylon or cotton-webbed collar. This collar should be adjustable so that it can be used for the first couple of months. A properly fit collar is tight enough that it will not slip over the head, yet an adult finger fits easily under it. A puppy should never wear a choke chain or any other adult training collar.

In addition to a collar, you'll need a 4-to-6-foot-long leash. One made of nylon or cotton-webbed material is a fine and inexpensive first leash. It does not need to be more than $1/2$-inch in width. It is important to make sure that the clip is of

HOUSEHOLD DANGERS

Curious puppies and inquisitive dogs get into trouble not because they are bad, but simply because they want to investigate the world around them. It's our job to protect our dogs from harmful substances, like the following:

In the Garage

antifreeze

garden supplies, like snail and slug bait, pesticides, fertilizers, mouse and rat poisons

In the House

cleaners, especially pine oil

perfumes, colognes, aftershaves

medications, vitamins

office and craft supplies

electric cords

chicken or turkey bones

chocolate, onions

some house and garden plants, like ivy, oleander and poinsettia

13

excellent quality and cannot become unclasped on its own.

EXERCISING YOUR SHIH TZU

By the time she is grown, your Shih Tzu will need to be exercised only

This puppy is safer now that she has an adjustable woven web collar and I.D. tag.

three times a day. A brisk walk around the block will provide sufficient exercise for her. These outings should take place on a regular schedule. Do not let your dog go outside off lead unless she is in a securely fenced yard, and do not leave her outside for hours unattended. No matter how well-trained your Shih Tzu might be, she might decide to wander away, disappear with a stranger or race across the street after a child or cat and get hit by a car.

Shih Tzu are basically not outdoor dogs and like to spend most of their time in the house. They also are not very well-suited to walks in the woods because their coats pick up leaves, sticks and burrs.

CHAPTER THREE

To Good Health

Today, the owner of a Shih Tzu is truly fortunate, and for many reasons. Given a reasonable level of consistent, attentive care, most Shih Tzu will enjoy at least a dozen happy years.

Another reason for the good fortune of today's Shih Tzu owner is one shared by all dog owners. Modern advances in veterinary science have done for our dogs what advances in human medicine have done for us.

Today, your Shih Tzu can look forward to a lifetime of better health care in both routine and unusual situations.

PREVENTIVE CARE

The easiest way to make sure your Shih Tzu remains healthy and sound is to make preventive care a priority from the start. This will require a minimal but essential amount of effort on your part, and will mean less money in vet bills and less heartache and discomfort for you and your Shih Tzu later on.

Choose a knowledgeable veterinarian, and establish a good working relationship with him or her. Follow the vaccination schedule you devise with your vet, and be sure to follow up with boosters when necessary. Examine your Shih Tzu from head to tail every day (and check for cuts, lumps and parasites) when you groom him.

Keeping your puppy's environment safe and clean will do much to minimize potential hazards. Keep your puppy on a leash or in an enclosed yard, and make sure he has some basic obedience training. This will help to make sure your pup heeds your commands when necessary. If you are trying to call him near a busy street, you need to be reasonably sure he won't tear off into oncoming traffic.

This Shih Tzu rests easy knowing that he is well cared for.

VACCINATIONS

One of the most important items on your agenda on the day you get your new Shih Tzu puppy is to get a copy of his health records. This will include the types and names of all inoculations, and when they were given, as well as a complete list of wormings. Take this to your veterinarian on your first visit, and she or he will set up a schedule to continue these inoculations.

The diseases your puppy needs to be vaccinated against include ditemper, hepatitis, parainfluenza and leptospirosis. All the diseases your puppy needs protection from have specific symptoms and means of transmission. Remember all these diseases are extremely serious (most are fatal) and they are all easily preventable with vaccinations.

Distemper is a viral disease and is highly contagious and is spread by canine urine and feces. An affected dog will run a high fever, cough, vomit, have diarrhea and seizures. These symptoms will worsen, ultimately leading to death.

Hepatitis is a most serious liver disorder characterized by fever, abdominal pain, vomiting and diarrhea.

YOUR PUPPY'S VACCINES

Vaccines are given to prevent your dog from getting infectious diseases like canine distemper or rabies. Vaccines are the ultimate preventive medicine: They're given before your dog ever gets the disease so as to protect him from the disease. That's why it is necessary for your dog to be vaccinated routinely. Puppy vaccines start at 8 weeks of age for the five-in-one DHLPP vaccine and are given every three to four weeks until the puppy is 16 months old. Your veterinarian will put your puppy on a proper schedule and will remind you when to bring in your dog for shots.

Parainfluenza, also known as "kennel cough," is not a particularly debilitating upper respiratory infection characterized by a dry, nonproductive cough, but it is extremely infectious. The mode of inoculation for parainfluenza is usually through the nostrils, with a specially adapted syringe tip. Because there are so many strains of this disease (much like the flu in humans), one vaccine cannot prevent them all. However, if you are planning on making any kind of trip to another location or will be boarding your puppy

Diseases aren't threatening these pups—they've had all their shots!

in a kennel facility, a parainfluenza shot is necessary.

Leptospirosis is a bacterial disease spread by the urine of infected animals. Mice and rats are especially implicated in transmission, so protection is a good idea. This is particularly important for Shih Tzu, since they will relentlessly seek out rats and mice in their environment. Pest control! It's a good idea to speak to the vet about this vaccination, since leptospirosis shots sometimes result in a bad reaction in the puppy.

Parvovirus and **coronavirus** have become noteworthy health problems among companion dogs. Both diseases are extremely infectious and spread by canine feces. Affected dogs

show a high fever and bloody and/or mucoid diarrhea. Their behavior is lethargic, and they are in great peril as these dangerous diseases are often fatal. Happily, there is protection against both these killers. Get your puppy inoculated, and keep him away from sickly looking dogs or places where many dogs congregate. Parvovirus in particular is extremely hardy and may survive in the environment for many months.

Dog owners are required by law to have their pets inoculated for **rabies.** This disease is characterized by altered behavior; shy animals may appear friendly or aggressive. As the virus spreads, the animal will begin to salivate excessively and drool. The virus is spread through the animal's saliva. There is no cure for rabies in dogs. People who have been bitten by a rabid animal must endure a long and painful series of shots. This is one vaccine that is not optional, with good reason!

Booster Shots

After your puppy gets his first permanent shot, he should have an annual booster. Always keep your Shih Tzu's shots current. You open a door to disaster for your pet when you let boosters slide.

INTERNAL PARASITES

There's no getting away from it—worms are a fact of life, but you can do a lot to make sure they don't cause problems for your Shih Tzu.

When you pick up your puppy, you should be given, along with the vaccination schedule, the dates of the puppy's previous wormings and the names of the drugs that were used. When you take your new puppy to the veterinarian for that first checkup, take his medical history, and take along a stool sample as well. The veterinarian will examine

it and determine what kind of worms, if any, are present. She or he will also give you the appropriate medicine and instruct you on the dosage.

In most cases, worming a puppy is a pretty straightforward matter, and today's medications are much easier on a puppy's delicate system than were the remedies of years ago. Don't ignore a worm infestation, but know that such conditions are not unusual and will respond to proper treatment.

Roundworms

These worms are extremely common and can infest even unborn puppies, passing through the placenta to establish themselves. In heavy infestations, it is not unusual to see live roundworms in a puppy stool. Roundworms can even be vomited up. They get their name by their tendency to curl up when exposed to air. Symptoms of roundworm infestation include a pot belly and a dull coat. Diarrhea and vomiting are other clues to the presence of these worms. Your veterinarian can dispense the right drugs to expel the pests, and you will probably need to repeat the dosage about ten days

Common internal parasites (l–r): roundworm, whipworm, tapeworm and hookworm.

later to break the worm's life cycle and get rid of worms that matured after your initial dosing. For puppies, roundworms can be especially serious, so if your puppy has them, act fast.

Tapeworm

Tapeworm is another common internal parasite and is usually spread by fleas, which act as intermediate hosts. A dog troubled with a flea infestation may swallow some fleas while biting at itchy flea bites, and in the process ingest tapeworm eggs. Tapeworms are long, segmented parasites, and the fresh, moving segments are often plainly visible in a stool. Dried segments stuck to the dog's hair near the anus resemble grains of brown rice. A tapeworm-affected dog may have diarrhea, dry skin or appear underweight. He may bite at his hindquarters or "scoot" them along the ground. Again, follow the veterinarian's directions and

remember to treat your dog and household surroundings for fleas.

Hookworm

Hookworm is a common cause of anemia and is particularly devastating to young puppies. The parasite gets a good foothold when hygienic conditions are not observed or when dogs are exposed to contaminated areas. A dog may swallow larvae, or the worm may penetrate the dog's skin. Eggs are identifiable through microscopic examination from a fresh stool sample. Your veterinarian can dispense drugs to combat hookworm, but it is also necessary to keep your surroundings clean and prevent the puppy from contact with feces and other animals.

Whipworm

Suspect whipworm if your dog is passing a watery or mucoid stool, shows weakness, weight loss, general symptoms of anemia or appears to be in overall poor condition. Whipworm is not visible to the naked eye, so determination of infestation is up to your veterinarian and his or her microscope. If your dog does have whipworm, you will probably have to have several stool checks done and institute a regimen of medication prescribed by your veterinarian.

Treating your dog for whipworm, by itself, is not enough. Whipworms, like so many other internal parasites, thrive in and are contracted from contaminated soil and unsanitary conditions. Sanitation and strict monitoring are important to keeping your dog clear of whipworm and all the other insidious parasites that can infest your dog.

Keeping your Shih Tzu free of internal parasites is another important aspect of health care.

Heartworm

The condition is passed by the bite of a mosquito infected with the heartworm larvae. It may take some time for the symptoms to show, and once the adult worms take up residence in your dog's heart, heroic measures may be needed to restore a dog's health.

It is far easier and wiser to use preventive measures to protect your Shih Tzu from heartworm infestation. Your veterinarian will draw a blood sample from your dog at the appropriate time and examine it under a microscope for heartworm microfilaria. In the probable event that your dog is negative for heartworm, your veterinarian will dispense the pills or syrup your dog needs to remain free of the parasite.

Suspect heartworm if your dog exhibits a chronic cough and a general weakness, with an unexplained loss of weight. If your dog tests positive, your veterinarian is the only person qualified to treat him.

Protozoans

Not all internal parasites are worms. Tiny, single-celled organisms called protozoans can also wreak havoc in your Shih Tzu's internal mechanisms, but effective treatment is available. The most common disorders in dogs caused by protozoans are coccidiosis and giardiasis.

Coccidiosis is generally the result of poor hygienic conditions in the dog's surroundings. The symptoms of this inflammation of the intestinal tract include sometimes bloody diarrhea, a generally poor appearance, cough, runny eyes and nasal and eye discharges. The disease is more serious in puppies, who are less resistant.

While grooming your pet, check the condition of his skin.

22

Giardiasis comes from drinking water contaminated with the disease-causing organism (usually from a stream). Giardia is nicknamed "beaver fever" because the organism is be spread by beavers that relieve themselves in lakes and streams. As with coccidiosis, diarrhea—the color of milk chocolate—is the symptom to watch for. A veterinarian must make the definite diagnosis.

EXTERNAL PARASITES

Fleas

For your Shih Tzu, a good scratch is one of life's little pleasures. However, if your Shih Tzu appears to be spending a lot of time scratching himself and doing so with a vengeance, you should take a closer look. If your Shih Tzu's skin looks red and irritated and there are little dark flecks throughout his coat, fleas may have set up housekeeping with your pet as their primary host. Bad news? Absolutely, but there are things you can do about it.

First, treat your dog. He should be dipped and given a good bath with a flea and tick shampoo. Be cautious here as some preparations will turn a Shih Tzu's coat pink. Luckily, nowadays there are several easy-to-administer systematic treatments (available from your vet), which make your dog flea-free.

Getting the fleas off your Shih Tzu alone is not enough. You must also treat your home and yard. Destroy any contaminated bedding, and go over the dog's entire environment with a spray or fogger to kill all the fleas. This means outdoors as well as inside the home. And even with all this, you must exercise common sense in other matters regarding flea control.

Ticks

Ticks look like tiny spiders. They attach themselves to a passing dog, suck blood from the dog, mate, and drop off, and the females lay thousands of eggs to begin the life cycle yet again. In the course of feeding, the female, which is much larger than the male, becomes engorged with blood. As with fleas, you must rid your dog and your environment of ticks if your control is to be effective.

Ticks are not as active as fleas, so removing them is a little easier. Gently but thoroughly comb your dog each time you return home from

FLEAS AND TICKS

There are so many safe, effective products available now to combat fleas and ticks that—thankfully—they are less of a problem. Prevention is key, however. Ask your veterinarian about starting your puppy on a flea/tick repellent right away. With this, regular grooming and environmental controls, your dog and your home should stay pest-free. Without this attention, you risk infesting your dog and your home, and you're in for an ugly and costly battle to clear up the problem.

23

a walk during tick season. Go over the entire dog with a pair of tweezers; do not attempt to remove ticks with your fingers. Shih Tzu owners unlucky enough to have to deal with ticks can take comfort from the fact that the white coat makes it easier to find the little vampires. When you find a tick, drip a little alcohol directly on it. The alcohol will asphyxiate the tick, causing it to release its hold. Pull it off with tweezers, and drop the tick into a small cup of alcohol, where it will drown and trouble your dog no more. Diligence is the watchword with tick control. Once you've gotten rid of the ticks, during tick season

ADVANTAGES OF SPAY/NEUTER

The greatest advantage of spaying (for females) or neutering (for males) your dog is that you are guaranteed your dog will not produce puppies. There are too many puppies already available for too few homes. There are other advantages as well.

Advantages of Spaying

No messy heats.

No "suitors" howling at your windows or waiting in your yard.

No risk of pyometra (disease of the uterus) and decreased incidences of mammary cancer.

Advantages of Neutering

Decreased incidences of fighting, but does not affect the dog's personality.

Decreased roaming in search of bitches in season.

Decreased incidences of many urogenital diseases.

keep your dog out of those wild, woodsy places where ticks hide, waiting for your unsuspecting Shih Tzu to come along and be their meal ticket.

In checking your Shih Tzu for ticks, pay particular attention to the face, the base of the ears, between the toes and the skin around the rear end—all places ticks seem to congregate.

Mites

Mites infest different areas of a dog's body. You might say the various species are specialists of a sort.

The **ear mite** *(Otodectes cynotis)* is a common problem for dogs with dropped ears, but even Shih Tzu with their erect ears can be troubled by them. If your Shih Tzu seems constantly to be scratching at his ears and if, on examination, you notice a dark, crumbly, malodorous accumulation, your dog has ear mites and must be treated for them. Your veterinarian can give you medication and instructions for clearing up the problem.

Scabies, or sarcoptic mange, is yet another condition related to mite infestation. The causative agent, *Sarcoptes scabei,* is a microscopic organism that burrows under the host's skin, causing intense itching and hair loss. This condition can also be passed to humans. Left untreated, it can spread to a dog's entire body.

Demodetic mange is the name of the condition spread by *Demodex* canis. The mite lives in the dog's hair follicles, causing hair loss and red, thickened skin. Eventually pustules form in infected follicles. Diagnosis via skin scrapings is required, and medicated dips are the treatment of choice to destroy these mites.

FIRST AID AND EMERGENCY CARE

Life for our dogs, as for us, always involves uncertainty. That is why you need to have some ability to minister to your dog in the event of a sudden illness or injury.

Muzzling

The first thing you should know how to do is to handle and transport an injured animal safely. A dog in pain is probably not going to recognize his owner or realize that people are trying to help him. In those circumstances, he is likely to bite. The dog in trouble needs to be muzzled.

Transporting Your Dog in an Emergency

An emergency stretcher can be made from a blanket and, depending on the size of the dog, carried by two or more people. An injured dog can also be carried on a rigid board, in a box or wrapped in a towel and carried in a person's arms. Care should be taken, though, that the manner of transport does not exacerbate the dog's original injury.

Shock

If a dog is in shock, keep him as warm and as quiet as possible and get him emergency veterinary attention at once.

Bleeding

If your dog is bleeding, direct pressure is an effective way to staunch the flow. You can fashion a pressure dressing from gauze or some strong fabric. Wrap the area of the wound, applying even pressure as you apply the gauze strips. If you notice tissue swelling below the site of the wound, ease the pressure or, if necessary, remove the bandage altogether. If you have no gauze, use any clean cloth or your hand as a last resort. For arterial bleeding, you will probably need a tourniquet along with the pressure bandage. You may use gauze strips, cloth or any other material that can

25

WHEN TO CALL THE VETERINARIAN

In any emergency situation, you should call your veterinarian immediately. Try to stay calm when you call, and give the vet or the assistant as much information as possible before you leave for the clinic. That way, the staff will be able to take immediate, specific action when you arrive. Emergencies include:

- Bleeding or deep wounds
- Hyperthermia (overheating)
- Shock
- Dehydration
- Abdominal pain
- Burns
- Fits
- Unconsciousness
- Broken bones
- Paralysis

Call your veterinarian if you suspect any health troubles.

be wrapped tightly between the wound and the heart to slow the flow of blood. With a tourniquet, you must remember to loosen the pressure about every ten minutes. Get the injured dog to a veterinarian as soon as possible.

Diarrhea

Diarrhea is often the normal result of your dog having eaten something he shouldn't have. However, it can also be the symptom of something more serious, and in young puppies, it can cause dehydration quickly. If diarrhea continues for more than twenty-four hours, or if you notice any other symptoms, call your vet immediately.

Heatstroke

The Shih Tzu's system is admirably suited to the cold, but far less efficient in heat. Dogs can die from heatstroke easily. Regardless of the season, a dog showing signs of heat distress—rapid, shallow breathing and a rapid heartbeat—needs to be cooled down immediately. Spraying or soaking the dog with cold water, or pressing an ice bag or freezer pack against the groin, abdomen, anus, neck and forehead are all effective in bringing down the stricken dog's temperature.

Choking

If your Shih Tzu is choking, you must act quickly to find and dislodge the foreign object after securing the mouth open by inserting a rigid object between the molars on one side. Use your fingers or, very carefully, use long-nosed pliers or a hemostat to withdraw the object. The Heimlich maneuver can also be used for choking dogs; ask your veterinarian to demonstrate how it's done.

Lameness

A Shih Tzu can go lame for a wide variety of reasons. He can cut a pad, pick up a foreign body (like a thorn) or break a nail. All these things will cause lameness. For cuts, clean the area and apply an antiseptic. If the wound is deep, staunch the bleeding and get your Shih Tzu to the vet. Also, for a painful broken nail, visit your veterinarian as soon as possible. He or she will medicate the injury to promote healing. With a broken nail, the vet will trim off as much as possible and cauterize and wrap the dog's paw.

Insect Bites

If your Shih Tzu is bitten by any stinging insect, remove the stinger,

Keep a watchful eye on your Shih Tzu's behavior. If you notice any changes, your pet might not be feeling well.

WHAT'S WRONG WITH MY DOG?

We've listed some common symptoms of health problems and their possible causes. If any of the following symptoms appear serious or persist for more than 24 hours, make an appointment to see your veterinarian immediately.

CONDITIONS	POSSIBLE CAUSES
DIARRHEA	Intestinal upset, typically caused by eating something bad or overeating. Can also be a viral infection, a bad case of nerves or anxiety or a parasite infection. If you see blood in the feces, get to the vet right away.
VOMITING/RETCHING	Dogs regurgitate fairly regularly (bitches for their young), whenever something upsets their stomachs, or even out of excitement or anxiety. Often dogs eat grass, which, because it's indigestible in its pure form, irritates their stomachs and causes them to vomit. Getting a good look at *what* your dog vomited can better indicate what's causing it.
COUGHING	Obstruction in the throat; virus (kennel cough); roundworm infestation; congestive heart failure.
RUNNY NOSE	Because dogs don't catch colds like people, a runny nose is a sign of congestion or irritation.
LOSS OF APPETITE	Because most dogs are hearty and regular eaters, a loss of appetite can be your first and most accurate sign of a serious problem.
LOSS OF ENERGY (LETHARGY)	Any number of things could be slowing down your dog, from an infection to internal tumors to overexercise—even overeating.

apply a baking soda paste to the affected area and stop the swelling and pain with an ice bag or cold pack. It would be a wise idea to run your pet's wounds past your vet to be sure all is well. An antibiotic may be prescribed.

CONDITIONS	POSSIBLE CAUSES
STINKY BREATH	Imagine if you never brushed your teeth! Foul-smelling breath indicates plaque and tartar buildup that could possibly have caused infection. Start brushing your dog's teeth.
LIMPING	This could be caused by something as simple as a hurt or bruised pad, to something as complicated as hip dysplasia, torn ligaments or broken bones.
CONSTANT ITCHING	Probably due to fleas, mites or an allergic reaction to food or environment (your vet will need to help you determine what your dog's allergic to).
RED, INFLAMED, ITCHY SPOTS	Often referred to as "hot spots," these are particularly common on coated breeds. They're caused by a bacterial infection that gets aggravated as the dog licks and bites at the spot.
BALD SPOTS	These are the result of excessive itching or biting at the skin so that the hair follicles are damaged; excessively dry skin; mange; calluses; and even infections. You need to determine what the underlying cause is.
STINKY EARS/HEAD SHAKING	Take a look under your dog's ear flap. Do you see brown, waxy buildup? Clean the ears with something soft and a special cleaner, and don't use cotton swabs or go too deep into the ear canal.
UNUSUAL LUMPS	Could be fatty tissue, could be something serious (infection, trauma, tumor). Don't wait to find out.

Bee stings are painful, but even more serious is the possibility that your dog is allergic to them. If so, the sting will start to swell immediately. If this happens, get your Shih Tzu to the vet as soon as possible. He or she will administer an antihistamine or other treatment.

POISON ALERT

If your dog has ingested a potentially poisonous substance, waste no time. Call the National Animal Poison Control Center hot line:

(800) 548-2423 ($30 per case) or

(900) 680-0000 ($20 first five minutes; $2.95 each additional minute)

Vomiting

This owner is cleaning out her Shih Tzu's ear canal in order to prevent infection.

Your dog will regurgitate when he eats something he shouldn't have, and this is usually nothing to worry about. However, if the vomitus looks bloody or otherwise unusual, call your

vet immediately. If your dog has been throwing up, you may want to help him along to recovery by feeding a bland diet of moist rice with a little chicken. You may want to add a tablespoon of yogurt to help restore helpful microbes to the digestive tract. If your dog vomits more than once, take him to the veterinarian.

CARE OF THE EARS

The Shih Tzu, like other breeds with dropped and hairy ears, is more likely to develop ear problems because the ear gets little air. Cleaning the excess hair out of the ear canal (not the ear flap, where the hairs have nerve endings that make extraction painful) improves air circulation and helps to prevent infection.

CARE OF THE EYES

Because Shih Tzu have large eyes with shallow sockets, their eyes may be more prone to injury than those of some other breeds. If your dog's eyes are red or cloudy or tear excessively, or if your dog keeps squinting and rubbing at his eye, get him to your veterinarian immediately. If he has an injury or is developing an infection, prompt treatment can prevent scarring or possibly even the loss of an eye.

Short-faced dogs with shallow eye sockets, such as the Shih Tzu, are also more prone to traumatic proptosis, in which the eye is dislodged from the socket. The eyelids then close behind the eye, cutting off the supply of oxygen to the eye. Proptosis can cause blindness and the loss of the eye if not treated by a veterinarian within twenty minutes.

Among the hereditary eye problems found in Shih Tzu are juvenile cataracts and progressive retinal atrophy (PRA), both of which lead to blindness. Both diseases are relatively rare in the breed, and a dog with either condition should never be bred.

Corneal Ulcers

These are the most serious eye problem commonly affecting Shih Tzu. An ulcer looks like a small dot on the dark part of the eye; the pupil may appear bluish, and the white of the eye is usually red and inflamed.

A corneal ulcer can be caused by irritation such as that caused by abnormally placed eyelashes or by

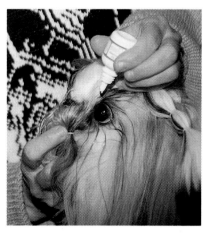

When a Shih Tzu's eyes are dry, irritated or infected, applying eye drops is a common remedy.

injury (be careful using the comb or brush around the eye). It may also occur spontaneously. An inability of the dog to properly close his eyelid over the cornea, or "dry eye," can cause chronic ulceration and may require daily eyedrops for the life of your dog.

If your dog has or is developing a corneal ulcer, prompt treatment is essential. An untreated ulcer can cause the cornea to rupture. See your veterinarian at once.

PROBLEMS ASSOCIATED WITH A SHORT FACE

The short face of the Shih Tzu can contribute to various health problems

Your short-faced Shih Tzu can overheat while playing outside in the heat.

because its anatomical conformation compresses the nasal cavity, pharynx, larynx and surrounding tissues into a small space. Shih Tzu puppies may snore, snort, bubble or sniffle, particularly while teething. These

Give your Shih Tzu some hard chewtoys to help him strengthen his teeth and gums.

symptoms are no cause for concern if the nasal discharge is clear and the dog is thriving.

Slightly pinched nostrils are very common in this breed and normally correct themselves as the dog matures. If your dog's nostrils are extremely pinched, so he can only breathe through his mouth and has trouble eating, even after he has cut his adult teeth, you may wish to have him examined by a specialist.

It is important to be sure that your short-faced Shih Tzu does not become overheated. Do not leave him in a car with the windows closed or take him for long walks outdoors when the weather is hot. Blue ice packs will help keep your dog cool when you travel in the "dog days" of summer.

CARE OF THE TEETH AND GUMS

The Shih Tzu's undershot bite frequently causes him to lose some of his front teeth at an early age. Missing or unaligned teeth or retained baby teeth are quite common in the breed.

To prevent tooth decay and gum disease, give your dog kibble, dog biscuits and hard toys to chew on and have your veterinarian show you how to clean your dog's teeth. If tartar and plaque build up, you may have to have your veterinarian scale your dog's teeth under anesthesia, so it is best to make dental care part of your regular routine. Neglected teeth and gums can lead to infection and cause serious health problems for your dog later in life.

HEREDITARY PROBLEMS OF THE SHIH TZU

Every breed of dog has some sort of breed or type-specific disorder. Some breeds are prone to more serious problems than others. However, none of this means that you must forego the pleasure of your chosen breed's companionship.

The Shih Tzu does present a number of health concerns, but in general this is a trouble-free breed and most Shih Tzu live to a ripe old age.

RENAL DYSPLASIA

Renal dysplasia, a developmental defect of the kidneys, is the most serious inherited disorder found in Shih Tzu. It is also present in Lhasa Apsos and, less frequently, in some

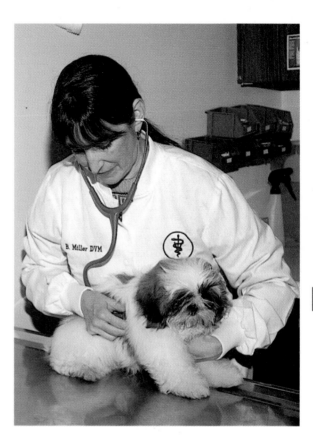

other breeds. In renal dysplasia, a varying number of nephrons (urine-forming units) in the kidneys never mature and some may be replaced with fibrous tissue.

Severely affected puppies drink and urinate excessively and are smaller than normal. Rather quickly they begin to vomit, become weak, debilitated and dehydrated and ultimately die of kidney failure. Moderately

Regular veterinary visits are a surefire way to detect any genetic diseases in your Shih Tzu.

affected puppies may appear normal until 5 or 6 months of age and then follow the same course.

Only a small percentage of Shih Tzu are severely affected by renal dysplasia and will die of renal failure. Affected dogs should never be bred because slightly affected dogs can live a normal life with normal renal function while still passing along some degree of the defect to their offspring.

Stones

Shih Tzu may be affected with kidney or bladder stones. Symptoms of bladder stones include urinary blockage, painful voiding, blood in the urine and cystitis. Large stones are generally removed surgically. Smaller stones can be dissolved and new stones kept from forming with a special diet prescribed by your veterinarian. Infections and other types of obstructions may cause similar symptoms, all of which should be treated promptly by your veterinarian.

Portal Systemic Shunt

This is another inherited disease that may be found, in rare instances, in Shih Tzu and several other smaller breeds. In this condition, blood is diverted around the liver into the bloodstream without being detoxified. Many cases are diagnosed in young animals. Those affected are depressed, thin and have trouble gaining weight. They may periodically exhibit peculiar behavior, such as bouts of aggression, staggering, pacing, circling, head pressing, blindness, deafness, tremors and seizures. Your veterinarian can test for the presence of the condition and provide a special diet. The defect can be surgically corrected; without surgery, severely affected animals probably will die of liver failure.

Hernias

Small umbilical hernias are frequently found in Shih Tzu puppies. These are almost always inherited; consequently, affected dogs, their litter mates and their parents should not be bred! Unless they are very large, umbilical hernias usually close by themselves. Inguinal hernias, found in the groin area, are much more serious. Many will require surgical correction, and dogs with inguinal hernias should not be bred.

Hypothyroidism

Hypothyroidism is a deficiency in the production of the hormones from the thyroid gland. Such a deficiency causes hair to become brittle and fall out easily. The dog's skin will also get thick and turn a darker color. Thyroid also controls metabolism, and a dog with hypothyroidism will be lethargic, tend to be fat and will have limited energy. The deficiency can range from mild to severe; mild cases may not even appear to be present, though a blood test can determine it.

Bone and Joint Disorders

Like other breeds, Shih Tzu may inherit hip dysplasia and other bone and joint disorders such as spinal disk problems and slipping kneecaps. Although such diseases in small breeds generally tend not to be crippling, they can be very painful. If you plan to breed your dog, first have it certified by the Orthopedic Foundation for Animals. Lameness in elderly dogs may be caused by arthritis.

CHAPTER FOUR

Positively Nutritious

Dog owners take their pets to the veterinarian when they become ill, to the groomer for a special occasion or to a training session when the spirit moves them. However, they feed their pets every single day. What they are fed, when they are fed and how they are fed are of great importance.

Over the course of a dog's life, her nutritional requirements will change just as ours do, and it is important to be aware of those needs ahead of time. If you approach the entire matter of feeding from a commonsense point of view and arm yourself with good information, you can expect that your dog will be properly fed for her entire life.

FEEDING YOUR SHIH TZU PUPPY

If you are about to get your first Shih Tzu, you will surely want to know just what to do to make sure you feed her properly. Before you bring her home, ask the breeder what she is being fed and when, and stick to the same food and routine after you get her home. Do this for at least the first week or so.

In most cases, the puppy you get will be on three meals a day. Stick to this number of feedings as much as possible.

The three-meals-a-day routine should be followed until the puppy reaches about 6 months of age. At

GROWTH STAGE FOODS

Once upon a time, there was puppy food and there was adult dog food. Now there are foods for puppies, young adults/active dogs, less active dogs and senior citizens. They vary by the amounts of nutrients they provide for the dog's growth stage/activity level. Less active dogs don't need as much protein or fat as growing, active dogs; senior dogs don't need some of the nutrients vital to puppies. By feeding a high-quality food that's appropriate for your dog's age and activity level, you're benefiting both of you. Feed too much protein to a couch potato, she'll have energy to spare; a few more trips around the block will be needed to burn it off. Feed an adult diet to a puppy and risk growth and development abnormalities that could last a lifetime.

A Shih Tzu who is eating a balanced diet is in good spirits, has lots of energy and has healthy skin and coat.

In order to compensate for the massive amount of energy they expend, puppies and adolescent Shih Tzu require a higher caloric intake than adult dogs.

TO SUPPLEMENT OR NOT TO SUPPLEMENT?

If you're feeding your dog a diet that's correct for her developmental stage and she's alert, healthy looking and neither over- nor underweight, you don't need to add supplements. These include table scraps as well as vitamins and minerals. Educating yourself about the quantity of vitamins and minerals your dog needs to be healthy will help you determine what needs to be supplemented. If you have any concerns about the nutritional quality of the food you're feeding, discuss them with your veterinarian.

this point, put her on a morning and an evening meal until she reaches her first birthday. At a year of age, she will do well on one meal a day, with biscuits in the morning and at bedtime. However, if you prefer to keep your Shih Tzu on two meals a day, there is no reason not to.

WHAT TO FEED YOUR SHIH TZU

Today, we and our dogs benefit from extensive research that has been conducted to find the best foods available for routine, day-to-day feeding, as well as foods for growing puppies, geriatrics, dogs with specific health needs and dogs with high levels of activity. The various dog food companies have gone to considerable expense to develop nutritionally complete, correctly balanced diets for all dogs.

Dry Food (Kibble)

The basis of your dog's diet should be dry kibble. A high-quality, well-balanced kibble is nutritionally complete and will be relished by your dog under all normal conditions. Most major dog food companies manufacture a special formulation to meet the explosive growth of young puppies. These are highly recommended for daily feeding up to your Shih Tzu's first birthday. Use the puppy foods. They work! For a mature dog, choose a kibble with a minimum of 20 percent protein. This and other important nutritional information will be on the label.

Many experienced dog keepers are firm believers in feeding dry kibble, or just flavoring it slightly with broth or canned meat to heighten palatability. Others, just as adamantly, insist that the dog is a natural meat eater and her diet should contain significant amounts

FOOD ALLERGIES

If your puppy or dog seems to itch all the time for no apparent reason, she could be allergic to one or more ingredients in her food. This is not uncommon, and it's why many foods contain lamb and rice instead of beef, wheat or soy. Have your dog tested by your veterinarian, and be patient while you strive to identify and eliminate the allergens from your dog's food (or environment).

of fresh or canned meat. Actually, a diet that mixes both meat and kibble is likely to provide your dog with the best features of both foods. If

39

Always have cool, fresh water available to your Shih Tzu.

HOW TO READ THE DOG FOOD LABEL

With so many choices on the market, how can you be sure you are feeding the right food to your dog? The information is all there on the label—if you know what you're looking for.

Look for the nutritional claim right up top. Is the food "100 percent nutritionally complete"? If so, it's for nearly all life stages; "growth and maintenance," on the other hand, is for early development; puppy foods are marked as such, as are foods for senior dogs.

Ingredients are listed in descending order by weight. The first three or four ingredients will tell you the bulk of what the food contains. Look for the highest-quality ingredients, like meats and grains, to be among them.

The Guaranteed Analysis tells you what levels of protein, fat, fiber and moisture are in the food, in that order. While these numbers are meaningful, they won't tell you much about the quality of the food. Nutritional value is in the dry matter, not the moisture content.

In many ways, seeing is believing. If your dog has bright eyes, a shiny coat, a good appetite and a good energy level, chances are her diet's fine. Your dog's breeder and your veterinarian are good sources of advice if you're still confused.

one had to come down on the side of one food or the other, the winner would have to be an all-kibble diet. Studies have shown that dogs raised on all-meat diets often suffer from malnutrition and serious deficiencies, which may cause extreme physically debilitating problems.

Water

Besides feeding a high-quality food, you must keep ample clean, fresh water available for your dog at all times. It is vital to do so.

ESTABLISHING A FEEDING SCHEDULE

Establishing a feeding schedule depends on the demands of your own daily routine. Whatever time you decide, feed at the same time every day. Dogs are creatures of habit and are happiest when maintained on a specific schedule. Of course, there will be days when you can't be there to feed your pet at her regular dinner hour. It's okay. An occasional break in the routine is not a disaster, as long as your dog knows that most of the time she will be fed at a set time.

How Much to Feed Your Shih Tzu

The amount of food you feed your Shih Tzu depends on the individual dog: her age, health, stage of life and activity level.

If your Shih Tzu is very active, she will burn more calories and need more food than a house pet who doesn't get extraordinary amounts of exercise. There will be a difference in the eating patterns of a growing puppy and an elderly animal. If your dog is ill or convalescing, her food needs will also differ from the requirements of a healthy animal. Use your own educated judgment.

If a healthy dog cleans her bowl but still appears hungry, she might need a little more to reach the right amount of daily ration. Adjust accordingly.

Another way to determine whether you are feeding the right amount of food is to let the dog's condition tell you. If your dog is healthy but appears thin, you may want to feed a bit more. If the dog looks to be on the plump side, a more restricted diet is in order. If you can't feel your dog's ribs beneath her fur, she's overweight. Weigh your dog, get your vet's advice and start her on a diet right away.

The Picky Eater

A healthy dog will eat food when it's offered and most of the time will clean the dish. If you know your Shih Tzu is healthy, but she consistently refuses to eat the good food you put in front of her, don't get into the habit of pampering her by offering alternative foods. This will only stiffen her resolve. Feed her at the same time and in the same quiet place every day. Leave the food down for five minutes and then remove it

Offering treats to your Shih Tzu is a great way to add a little variety to her diet!

A Shih Tzu begs relentlessly for some of what her owner is eating.

entirely, whether she has eaten or not. Don't worry, a healthy dog will eat before she starves.

PEOPLE FOOD

It can be okay to offer human food at times and to add table scraps

occasionally to your dog's food, but do it wisely and in moderation. Dogs like carrots, broccoli and other fresh vegetables; some even like fruits. These are okay, as are bits of cooked meat (no bones). And remember all those balanced rations mentioned earlier in this chapter: Quality food made specifically for dog feeding will do a better job of nourishing your pet than treats you may feel good about offering.

BONES

On the matter of bones, your Shih Tzu is infinitely better off without them. Certain beef bones are safe enough, but others, such as poultry, chop or fish bones, are definitely dangerous and should never be offered. If you need another reason to keep bones away from your Shih Tzu, think of what a greasy mess a Shih Tzu who has been playing with a big soup bone can become—it's not pretty, and there are many safe chewing items you can give your Shih Tzu that she will enjoy every bit as much.

CHAPTER FIVE

Putting on the Dog

Every time a novice owner looks at a beautiful Shih Tzu in the show-ring with coat dragging on the ground, the first question is, "What do I have to do to get such a gorgeous coat on my pet?" To a great extent, a profuse coat is inherited. Even more important, the coat is cared for carefully and regularly, and this care begins when you first bring your puppy home. The real key to a beautiful coat is regular brushing, so large mats

When it comes to grooming, Shih Tzu are high-maintenance dogs—but well worth the effort!

never have a chance to form, plus a bath at least once every three weeks. Because a dirty coat mats much more rapidly than a clean one, many show dogs are bathed every week.

BASIC GROOMING SUPPLIES

Before you begin, you will need the following supplies, which can be obtained from your local pet shop or a pet-supply catalog.

1. A pin brush with very flexible metal pins for basic grooming and a soft slicker brush.

2. A 7¹/₂-inch comb (preferably Teflon-coated) with wide and narrow tooth placement for face and feet and for checking for mats after brushing.

3. A comb with rotating teeth or a rake with two rows of teeth set into a wooden handle in a V shape for removing large and stubborn mats. Note that both of these tools

remove a lot of hair and are not recommended for show coats.

4. Pint-sized spray bottle (for water mixed with 1 teaspoon conditioner to mist coat before brushing).

5. Latex bands and colored bows for topknots.

6. Blunt-end scissors (for removing topknot bands and trimming sensitive areas) and straight-bladed 7-to-8-inch stainless-steel grooming shears for trimming.

7. Knitting needle or comb with needle (for parts and topknots).

8. Cat or human toenail clippers (for small puppies) and canine nail clippers (for older dogs); styptic powder (to halt bleeding if you cut a nail too short).

9. Ear powder and tweezers or ear hemostat (optional) for removing excess hair from inside the ear canal.

10. A good-quality dryer (preferably a freestanding table or stand model).

11. A high-quality shampoo and conditioner (see comments below under "Which Shampoos to Use?"), plus tearless shampoo for the face.

BASIC GROOMING

The first thing you must do is to get your new puppy used to being groomed regularly. It is best to begin by brushing your puppy in your lap every day, preferably when he is a bit tired and therefore likely to remain calm. Make grooming a loving time.

A pin brush (like the one this woman uses) is great for gathering loose hairs from your Shih Tzu's lustrous coat.

45

his world. Be sure the water is neither too hot nor too cold (test it on your wrist), and try not to frighten him by soaking his face with water.

BRUSHING TECHNIQUES

Brush gently and carefully in layers, beginning with the feet, legs and belly and working your way up to the center of the back. Because static electricity in a dry coat contributes to breakage, dampen the coat slightly first with the cream rinse and water mix in your spray bottle and brush in long, even strokes. Lift the top of the brush away at the end of each stroke rather than turning it into the coat and flipping the bottom of the brush up, which catches and breaks the ends of the coat. *Be sure to brush all the way down to the skin.*

If you encounter a mat, don't rip at it. Break it apart with your fingers before gently brushing out the dead hair. Large and stubborn mats will be easier to remove if you saturate them with cream rinse and wait a few moments before breaking them up. In extreme cases, the rotating-toothed comb or rake recommended above can be used for dematting.

Examining and cleaning your Shih Tzu's eyes as part of your regular grooming program can help prevent infections.

Clean your puppy's face every day and cut his nails and trim the hair between the pads of his feet at least every two weeks, so he will have firm footing as his muscles develop. Try to make his first baths pleasurable experiences, so bathing, like grooming, becomes a normal part of

How often you will need to brush an adult dog will depend on the texture of his coat. Some Shih Tzu can be done only twice a week; others must be done every day.

BEYOND BRUSHING

Once you have thoroughly brushed out your dog, use the knitting needle or parting comb to make a part down the center of the back and run the narrow-toothed end of your comb through the whiskers, holding the dog's head still by grasping his beard.

It is much safer to use a comb than a brush around the eyes. If your dog accumulates a lot of matter in the corners of his eyes, you may want to wash his face with a warm, soft cloth or wipe it with a damp cotton ball at this time. Then put up the topknot in a latex band, following the directions below.

TOPKNOTS

A puppy topknot is generally placed fairly low on the forehead in a single band to catch all the short hairs. Do not pull the hair up too tightly into the band or the dog will rub at it.

Later, you will want to do a double topknot to keep the hair from falling forward into the dog's eyes and to hold the topknot more securely.

This Shih Tzu sits calmly while his owner adjusts his topknot.

BATHING

Never bathe a matted dog. Brush out the dog thoroughly first. Bathing sets in mats like cement, making them

Step 1: Thoroughly wet down your Shih Tzu with tepid water.

Step 2: Apply shampoo to your dog's coat and work it up to a lather.

48

Step 3: Rinse your Shih Tzu carefully, trying not to get water in the eyes and ear canal.

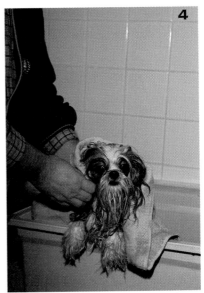

Step 4: Squeeze excess water from your dog's coat and towel dry.

almost impossible to remove. Before bathing, also check your dog's ears

and remove excess hair from the inside of the ear canal by pulling it out with your fingers or with tweezers or an ear hemostat; ear powder will make it easier to grip the hair. Such hair prevents proper air circulation in the ear canal and provides a moist breeding ground for infection.

WHICH SHAMPOOS TO USE?

Always use a tearless shampoo made specifically for canines on the face to avoid irritating the eyes, and try to avoid getting water in the eyes or into the ear canal. Do not use flea control products on the face.

Once your dog is in the tub and wet thoroughly with warm water, shampoo twice. The first soaping removes the cream rinse and surface dirt, and the second soaping gets the dog really clean.

Special whitener shampoos may help decrease the staining of white beards. Be very careful not to get such products into the eyes—a prebath drop of mineral oil in each eye will help to protect them.

After rinsing out the soap, put a capful or two of good conditioner into a quart of warm water and pour it over your dog, avoiding the face. Allow the conditioner to remain in the coat for a few minutes, then rinse.

POST-BATH PROCEDURES

Squeeze as much excess moisture as possible out of the coat, and wrap your dog in a couple of thick bath towels. Then hold him in your lap for ten or fifteen minutes, using a corner of one of the towels to wipe

Blow dry your Shih Tzu's coat with a warm heat, while gently brushing and straightening the coat.

49

QUICK AND PAINLESS NAIL CLIPPING

This is possible if you make a habit out of handling your dog's feet and giving your dog treats when you do. When it's time to clip nails, go through the same routine, but take your clippers and snip off just the ends of the nail—clip too far down and you'll cut into the "quick," the nerve center, hurting your dog and causing the nail to bleed. Clip two nails a session while you're getting your dog used to the procedure, and you'll soon be doing all four feet quickly and easily.

the face and blot the ears. You will find that this procedure dramatically reduces the amount of time your dog

This woman trims her Shih Tzu's toenails with a safety nail clipper.

spends under the dryer. While your dog is swaddled in towels is a good time to cut toenails. The toenails are also softer and easier to cut when wet. (See "Quick and Painless Nail Clipping" sidebar.)

DRYING YOUR DOG

Thoroughly dry your dog with a blow dryer set on warm—not hot, which could burn the skin. Pay special attention to the hair under the ears and on the back of the neck, which seem to take longest to dry.

Brush the dog gently while his coat dries to separate and straighten the hair and speed the drying process. You will find it easiest to use a dryer that leaves both of your hands free to work on the dog—particularly if the dog in question is a squirming puppy.

Once the dog is dry, give your pet a part and put up the topknot. Now is the time to trim the hair between the pads of the feet level with the footpads, so it will not collect dirt, knot and injure the tender skin. The hair on the top of the feet should be rounded, so the dog will not look like it has flippers.

If your dog's coat is long enough, comb it down and trim it level with the tabletop all the way around. This will remove split and uneven ends and make the coat look neater and fuller. Do not cut the hair on the muzzle short, even on a pet dog, because the short hairs will rub against the eye, possibly causing injury and most certainly increasing the amount of discharge from the eye that probably tempted you to cut it in the first place.

When you have finished, spray lightly with a little of your cream rinse and water mix or a coat-finishing product to keep the hair in place. Then put your Shih Tzu down and watch your pet prance—he enjoys looking good!

51

CUTTING YOUR DOG DOWN

If you have neither the time nor the inclination to keep up a long coat, it is much better for both you and your dog to keep him in a cute clip than to have you feeling guilty and your dog badly matted, unattractive and uncomfortable. You may want him trimmed short (1 to 2 inches) overall in what is commonly called a puppy clip, leaving only the hair on the ear leathers and tail and the moustache and beard long.

You may want to have your dog trimmed by a groomer every six to eight weeks. If you choose to do

A Shih Tzu having his foot pads trimmed.

This owner uses an electric dog clipper to achieve a puppy clip.

the job yourself, you will need good electric dog clippers with #10 or #7 blades, scissors and a slicker brush to keep pulling the hair out from the body while scissoring to achieve a smooth effect. When you clip or trim, be sure to begin with a clean, dry coat.

CHAPTER SIX

Measuring Up

The Shih Tzu has always been prized as a companion. Because of that, the dog's temperament is of the utmost importance. The Shih Tzu's unique head and expression distinguish the breed from two other related Oriental breeds, the Lhasa Apso and the Pekingese. Although the Shih Tzu is classified by the American Kennel Club (AKC) as a member of the Toy Group, the dog is solid and sturdy. Many consider the Shih Tzu to be a "big dog in a little package" in temperament and substance.

In both the pet and show dogs, correct temperament is equally important. Shih Tzu are alert, arrogant

54

THE SHIH TZU HEAD

Much of the breed standard is devoted to describing the head because this feature most distinguishes the breed. It is sometimes difficult to determine whether head and expression are correct simply by looking at them because skilled groomers can "do up" a topknot to make the head appear correct even when it is not.

When you think of the correct head and expression, think round, warm and soft. The head itself is large and round when viewed from the front or the side, and the ears are placed so that they appear to blend into the head. The eyes are also large and round, but they should not protrude. Although a small amount of eye white is acceptable, excessive eye white in the corners of the eye or around the entire eye or bulging eyes markedly detract from the desired warm, sweet expression, as does a lack of pigmentation on the nose, lips or eye rims. The eyes should be placed well apart, and the muzzle should be set no lower than the bottom of the eye rims.

The Shih Tzu is classified by the American Kennel Club as a member of the Toy Group.

and affectionate. They love people and other dogs, big and small. Everyone is this breed's friend. It is most unusual and highly undesirable for a Shih Tzu to be nasty, overly aggressive, nervous or shy.

The Shih Tzu breed standard describes the ideal specimen of the breed. Although the perfect dog has never been born, dog show judging is based on how closely each dog that is entered approaches the ideal picture described in the breed standard. The complete Official Standard of the breed is included for your reference.

The muzzle is short and square and unwrinkled—unlike the longer, narrower muzzle of the Lhasa Apso or the extremely short, wrinkled muzzle of the Pekingese. The muzzle should have good cushioning (fleshy padding), which contributes greatly to the soft expression. The jaw is undershot—that is, the lower jaw is longer than the upper jaw—although the teeth should not show when the mouth is closed, and the lower lip should not protrude when viewed from the side. The muzzle meets the foreskull at a definite angle (stop), giving the desired "pushed-in" look.

55

A SOLID, THOUGH SMALL, DOG

Good Shih Tzu are solid dogs that are surprisingly heavy for their size. Mature Shih Tzu ideally weigh between 9 and 16 pounds and stand no fewer than 8 inches and no more than 11 inches tall at the withers. Their length should be slightly longer from withers to base of tail than high at the withers. Most Shih Tzu in today's showrings measure slightly longer than high, although a wealth of hair may make the dogs appear shorter in back than they really are. The chest is broad and deep, there is good spring of rib and the legs are well boned and muscular.

The Shih Tzu's expression is soft and warm.

WHAT'S UNDER ALL THE HAIR?

The body of the Shih Tzu is short-coupled, with little distance between the last rib and the pelvis. There should never be the tuck-up found in breeds such as Afghan Hounds.

Can you believe a dog this small can weigh up to 16 pounds?!

In a Shih Tzu with the proper spring of rib and depth of chest, the rib cage should drop to just below the elbow. The chest should never be so wide that it forces the elbows out nor so narrow that the dog is slab-sided.

THE SHIH TZU'S BUILD

Structural soundness is as important in the Shih Tzu as it is in any other breed. A Shih Tzu with incorrect structure cannot possibly possess the smooth, flowing, effortless movement called for in the standard. One of the most common problem areas in this breed is poor fronts. The neck should flow smoothly into the shoulders, which should be well-angulated and well laid-back and fit smoothly into the body. Excessive development of muscles on the outside of the shoulder blade (loaded shoulders) or shoulders that lack in the desired angulation (straight shoulders) or that protrude from the topline and interrupt the smooth transition from the neck to the shoulders to the withers are undesirable. The shoulder blades should lie flat and toward the spine.

The front legs should be straight from the elbows to the pasterns and set well apart to support the broad deep chest. The elbows should be set close to the body, never out or loose, and the feet should point straight ahead. If the front legs are bowed or out at the elbows or the dog is barrel-chested, she will appear to roll like a Pekingese when moving toward you or to swing her legs out to the side and then in rather than extending them straight ahead. This makes for very inefficient and incorrect movement, as does toeing in or out.

CORRECT MOVEMENT

Front and rear angulation should be in balance for smooth movement, with good front reach and strong rear drive that are best evaluated by viewing the dog from the side. If both front and rear lack the correct angulation, the dog will move with a short, mincing stride, bobbing up and down instead of moving forward effortlessly. If the rear is more angulated

THE AMERICAN KENNEL CLUB

Familiarly referred to as "the AKC," the American Kennel Club is a nonprofit organization devoted to the advancement of purebred dogs. The AKC maintains a registry of recognized breeds and adopts and enforces rules for dog events including shows, obedience trials, field trials, hunting tests, lure coursing, herding, earth-dog trials, agility and the Canine Good Citizen program. It is a club of clubs, established in 1884 and composed, today, of over 500 autonomous dog clubs throughout the United States. Each club is represented by a delegate; the delegates make up the legislative body of the AKC, voting on rules and electing directors. The American Kennel Club maintains the Stud Book, the record of every dog ever registered with the AKC, and publishes a variety of materials on purebred dogs, including a monthly magazine, books and numerous educational pamphlets. For more information, contact the AKC at the address listed in chapter 9, "Resources."

than the front, the dog will sometimes move with a hackney gait, picking up her front legs excessively high to keep them out of the way of the on-coming back feet. A dog whose front and rear angulation are not in balance may also crab or sidewind, moving

The Shih Tzu has always been prized as a companion.

at a slight angle rather than straight forward to avoid having her rear legs interfere with her front ones. In general, a dog whose front and rear angulation are insufficient but in balance will look better when moving than one that has poor angulation in just the front or the rear. But lack of angulation in both front and rear involves two faults rather than just one.

The hind legs, like the front legs, should be well boned, muscular and set well apart in line with the forequarters. The hocks should be short enough to provide sufficient leverage for the desired strong, driving rear movement. Some Shih Tzu have luxating or double-jointed hocks. The tendons that hold the joints in place may be weak, causing them to buckle forward when gentle pressure is applied to the back of the joint. This is incorrect.

TOPS AND TAILS

When viewed from the side, the Shih Tzu should have a firm, level top-line, the head carried well up and the tail curved gently over the back in a "teacup handle."

THE SHIH TZU'S COAT

Another distinctive feature of the breed is the dog's long, flowing double coat, which may be slightly wavy but never curly. The double coat consists of a dense, soft undercoat and a somewhat harder outercoat. A sparse coat or a single coat (one without the desired undercoat) is undesirable. Because the coat is so profuse, it requires a great deal of grooming, although a coat of the correct sturdy texture requires much less care than an extremely soft, cottony coat and is much sought after.

The coat is parted in the center of the back, and the hair on the top of the head is tied into a topknot. The hair between the pads of the feet is cut short, and the feet are trimmed to give them a rounded appearance. Quite often the side coat is trimmed level with the ground, so the dog will not trip over it.

The Shih Tzu's most distinguishing features are her parted coat and topknots.

A RAINBOW OF SHIH TZU

The Shih Tzu comes in a variety of colors and markings, and all colors and markings are equally acceptable. Among the most common are gold and white, red and white, black and white, silver and white, brindle (a mixture of gold or silver and black) and white, solid gold or silver with a black mask and solid black. Less common, but also correct, are liver dogs, which have chocolate brown pigment and brown eyes, and blue dogs, which have gray-blue pigment and blue eyes.

Your pet will— and should— always be "Best in Show" in your eyes!

If you have purchased a pet Shih Tzu, chances are the dog possesses one or more faults based on the breed standard that make your pet unsuitable for the showring or for breeding. In the meantime, your dog can still be shown in obedience or agility. You might also want to train your dog to be a registered Therapy Dog and allow your pet to bring the same joy to others that she brings to you.

Most breeders are unwilling to sell an excellent show prospect to a home where the dog will not be shown. In many cases, however, the faults your dog has may be obvious only to someone involved in the show world and will go unnoticed by the average person. Whether or not your pet is an excellent representative according to the breed standard, the dog can still be an ideal companion and house pet. That is, after all, what Shih Tzu were bred for and why you purchased one.

OFFICIAL STANDARD FOR THE SHIH TZU

GENERAL APPEARANCE—The Shih Tzu is a sturdy, lively, alert Toy dog with a long, flowing double coat. Befitting his noble Chinese ancestry as a highly valued, prized companion and palace pet, the Shih Tzu is proud of bearing, has a distinctively arrogant carriage with head well up and tail curved over the back. Although there has always been considerable size variation, the Shih Tzu must be compact, solid, carrying good weight and substance. Even though a Toy dog, the Shih Tzu must be subject to the same requirements of soundness and structure prescribed for all breeds, and any deviation from the ideal described in the standard should be penalized to the extent of the deviation. Structural faults common to all breeds are as undesirable in the Shih Tzu as in any other breed, regardless of whether or not such faults are specifically mentioned in the standard.

SIZE, PROPORTION, SUBSTANCE— Size—Ideally, height at withers is 9 to 10½ inches, but no fewer than 8 inches nor more than 11. Ideally, weight of mature dogs, 9 to 16 pounds. Proportion—Length between withers and root of tail is slightly longer than height at withers. The Shih Tzu must never be so high stationed as to appear leggy, nor so low stationed as to appear dumpy or squatty. Substance— Regardless of size, the Shih Tzu is

WHAT IS A BREED STANDARD?

A breed standard—a detailed description of an individual breed—is meant to portray the ideal specimen of that breed. This includes ideal structure, temperament, gait, type—all aspects of the dog. Because the standard describes an ideal specimen, it isn't based on any particular dog. It is a concept against which judges compare actual dogs and breeders strive to produce dogs. At a dog show, the dog that wins is the one that comes closest, in the judge's opinion, to the standard for its breed. Breed standards are written by the breed parent clubs, the national organizations formed to oversee the well-being of the breed. They are voted on and approved by the members of the parent clubs.

always compact, solid and carries good weight and substance.

HEAD—Head—Round, broad, wide between eyes, its size in balance with the overall size of dog being neither too large nor too small. Fault: Narrow head, close-set eyes. Expression—Warm, sweet, wide-eyed, friendly and trusting. An overall well-balanced and pleasant expression supersedes the importance of individual parts. Care should be taken to look and examine well beyond

This Shih Tzu exhibits her round, wide eyes and broad, open nostrils.

the hair to determine if what is seen is the actual head and expression rather than an image created by grooming technique. Eyes—Large, round, not prominent, placed well apart, looking straight ahead. Very dark. Lighter on liver pigmented dogs and blue pigmented dogs. Fault: Small, close-set or light eyes; excessive eye white. Ears—Large, set slightly below crown of skull, heavily coated. Skull—Domed. Stop—There is a definite stop. Muzzle—Square, short, unwrinkled, with good cushioning, set no lower than bottom eye rim; never turned down. Ideally, no

longer than 1 inch from tip of nose to stop, although length may vary slightly in relation to overall size of dog. Front of muzzle should be flat; lower lip and chin not protruding and definitely never receding. Fault: Snippiness, lack of definite stop. Nose—Nostrils are broad, wide and open. Pigmentation—Nose, lips, eye rims are black on all colors, except liver on liver pigmented dogs and blue on blue pigmented dogs. Fault: Pink on nose, lips or eye rims. Bite—Undershot. Jaw is broad and wide. A missing tooth or slightly unaligned teeth should not be too severely penalized. Teeth and tongue should not show when mouth is closed. Fault: Overshot bite.

NECK, TOPLINE, BODY—Of utmost importance is an overall well-balanced dog with no exaggerated features. Neck—Well set-on flowing smoothly into shoulders; of sufficient length to permit natural high head carriage and in balance with height and length of dog. Topline—Level. Body—Short-coupled and sturdy with no waist or tuck-up. The Shih Tzu is slightly longer than tall. Fault: Legginess. Chest—Broad and deep with good spring-of-rib, however, not barrel-chested. Depth of rib cage should extend to just below elbow. Distance from elbow to withers is a little greater than from elbow to ground. Croup—Flat. Tail—Set on high, heavily plumed, carried in curve well over back. Too loose, too tight, too flat, or too low set a tail is undesirable and should be penalized to extent of deviation.

FOREQUARTERS—Shoulders—Well-angulated, well laid-back, well laid-in, fitting smoothly into body. Legs—Straight, well-boned, muscular, set well apart and under chest, with elbows set close to body. Pasterns—Strong, perpendicular. Dewclaws—May be removed. Feet—Firm, well padded, point straight ahead.

HINDQUARTERS—Angulation of hindquarters should be in balance with forequarters. Legs—Well-boned, muscular and straight when viewed from rear with well-bent stifles, not close set but in line with forequarters. Hocks—Well let down, perpendicular. Fault: Hyperextension of hocks. Dewclaws—May be removed. Feet—Firm, well padded, point straight ahead.

COAT—Luxurious, double-coated, dense, long and flowing. Slight wave permissible. Hair on top of head is tied up. Fault: Sparse coat, single coat, curly coat. Trimming—Feet, bottom of coat and anus may be done for

A profile of the Shih Tzu exemplifies the breed's double-coated, dense, long and flowing coat.

neatness and to facilitate movement. Fault: Excessive trimming.

COLOR AND MARKINGS—All are permissible and to be considered *equally.*

GAIT—The Shih Tzu moves straight and must be shown at its own natural speed, neither raced nor strung-up, to evaluate its smooth, flowing, effortless movement with good front reach and equally strong rear drive, level topline, naturally high head carriage and tail carried in gentle curve over back.

TEMPERAMENT—As the sole purpose of the Shih Tzu is that of companion and house pet, it is essential that its temperament be outgoing, happy, affectionate, friendly and trusting toward all.

CHAPTER SEVEN

A Matter of Fact

The Shih Tzu is one of several types of "Lion Dogs" whose ancestors developed in Asia at least as long ago as 1000 B.C. These breeds include the Shih Tzu, Lhasa Apso, Pug and Japanese Chin. The ancestors of the modern Shih Tzu may have been introduced to China from Tibet or Central Asia. Whatever their origin, our "chrysanthemum-faced" breed had an honored place in the Chinese court, particularly during the time of the Manchu Dynasty (1644–1911).

LITTLE LION DOGS

The name "Shih Tzu," pronounced "sheed-zoo," actually means "lion" in Chinese. Ancient scrolls showed short-legged dogs trimmed to resemble lions that had heavily bearded and moustached heads quite unlike the smooth-haired head of the

Pekingese. The breed's lionlike appearance gave the dog particular symbolic importance.

In Tibetan Buddhism, the lion was Buddha's steed and most important companion and, therefore, sacred. Lions were not indigenous to the Far East, however, so lionlike dogs assumed religious significance. Huge stone Lion Dogs guarded many temples and public buildings. Many of these Lion Dogs were in pairs, with the male resting his front foot on a ball and the female resting her foot on a puppy. Often they wore harnesses ornamented with tassels and bells and held ropes or ribbons in their mouths.

Lion Dogs were depicted on scrolls, and Lion-Dog statues were placed on household altars and ornamented the roof corners of temples, where they were thought to protect the temples from fire. Some of these Lion Dogs are ridden by Siddhartha Gautama, the founder of Buddhism, or by the Buddhist bodhisattva Manjusri, from whom the Manchu Dynasty took its name. Manjusri was said to have often been accompanied by a pet dog that could be transformed into a lion.

Among its attributes, the Chinese said that the Lion Dog was to have

dragon eyes, a lion head, a bear torso, a frog mouth, palm-leaf fan ears, a feather-duster tail and movement like a goldfish. Lion Dogs (known as Fo or Fu dogs and collected by many Shih Tzu owners) appear not only in Chinese art, but also in the art of Tibet, Japan, Korea, Thailand and Indonesia. Unlike the ferocious

Shih Tzu were considered sacred by the ancient Chinese.

65

FAMOUS OWNERS OF SHIH TZU

Zsa Zsa Gabor

Yul Brynner

Peggy Guggenheim

Paul Molitor

Elizabeth, Queen Consort of George VI

WHERE DID DOGS COME FROM?

It can be argued that dogs were right there at man's side from the beginning of time. As soon as human beings began to document their existence, the dog was among their drawings and inscriptions. Dogs were not just friends, they served a purpose: There were dogs to hunt birds, pull sleds, herd sheep, burrow after rats—even sit in laps! What your dog was originally bred to do influences the way he behaves. The American Kennel Club recognizes over 140 breeds, and there are hundreds more distinct breeds around the world. To make sense of the breeds, they are grouped according to their size or function. The AKC has seven groups:

1. Sporting
2. Working
3. Herding
4. Hounds
5. Terriers
6. Toys
7. Non Sporting

Can you name a breed from each group? Here's some help: (1) Golden Retriever; (2) Doberman Pinscher; (3) Collie; (4) Beagle; (5) Scottish Terrier; (6) Maltese; and (7) Dalmatian. All modern domestic dogs *(Canis familiaris)* are related, however different they look, and are all descended from *Canis lupus,* the gray wolf.

lion, the Lion Dogs are often smiling. Perhaps they reflect the ancient Shih Tzu's arrogant bearing and affectionate personality—or perhaps these attributes were selectively bred for long ago because of the breed's importance as both a religious symbol and a treasured companion.

OUT OF THE FAR EAST

The first Shih Tzu were taken from China to England, Ireland and Scandinavia in the late 1920s and early 1930s. Without these early exports, we would have no Shih Tzu today. The breed is believed to have become extinct in China after the Communists came to power in 1949 because the Communists considered pet dogs useless consumers of food and viewed them as a symbol of wealth and privilege.

EARLY AMERICAN IMPORTS

The first Shih Tzu were imported to the United States from England in 1938. Because the American Kennel Club did not yet recognize Shih Tzu as a separate breed, the earliest imports were bred and shown as Lhasa Apsos. The earliest American Shih Tzu descended from the English imports tended to have heavier bones, broader heads, shorter necks and denser coats than those coming down from the early imports from Scandinavia, which tended to have longer, straighter legs; narrower heads; finer bones; and silkier coats.

Some of the English-bred dogs had bowed front legs, thought to be the result of a controversial Shih Tzu–Pekingese cross performed by Elfreda Evans in 1952 that was later sanctioned by the English Kennel Club. Offspring of the Pekingese cross were allowed to be registered in Britain after three generations, but the American Kennel Club required six generations before it would allow Shih Tzu descended from the cross to be considered purebred. This delayed AKC recognition of the breed. Over time, the judicious crossing of the bloodlines led to the development of a truly American Shih Tzu, combining the best attributes of both types.

In 1955, Shih Tzu were admitted by the AKC to the Miscellaneous Class (the breed is now in the Toy Group), where they could compete for obedience titles but not in AKC-licensed conformation shows. From this time, the breed rapidly gained in popularity.

BOOMING IN POPULARITY

By 1969, some 3,000 Shih Tzu had been registered by the American Shih Tzu Club. Today the breed has become so popular that about as many Shih Tzu are registered with the American Kennel Club each month as were registered during the thirty-some years prior to AKC recognition.

Although in existence for centuries, the Shih Tzu only arrived in the United States about 60 years ago (most likely not in a handbasket).

In 1998, 38,468 Shih Tzu were registered with the American Kennel Club, ranking the Shih Tzu eleventh of all registered breeds.

CHAPTER EIGHT

On Good Behavior

by Ian Dunbar, Ph.D., MRCVS

T raining is the jewel in the crown— the most important aspect of doggy husbandry. There is no more important variable influencing dog behavior and temperament than the dog's education: A well-trained, well-behaved and good-natured puppydog is always a joy to live with, but an untrained and uncivilized dog can be a perpetual nightmare. Moreover, deny the dog an education and she will not have the opportunity to fulfill her own canine potential; neither will she have the ability to communicate effectively with her human companions.

Luckily, modern psychological training methods are easy, efficient, effective and, above all, considerably dog-friendly and user-friendly. Doggy education is as simple as it is enjoyable. But before you can have a good time play-training with your new dog, you have to learn what to do and how to do it. There is no bigger variable influencing the success of dog training than the owner's experience and expertise. Before you embark on the dog's education, you must first educate yourself.

BASIC TRAINING FOR OWNERS

Ideally, basic owner training should begin well before you select your dog. Find out all you can about your chosen breed first, then master rudimentary training and handling skills. If you already have your puppydog, owner training is a dire emergency—the clock is ticking! Especially for puppies, the first few weeks at home are the most important and influential days in the dog's life. Indeed, the cause of most adolescent and adult problems may be traced back to the initial days the pup explores her new home. This is the time to establish the *status quo*—to teach the puppydog how you would like her to behave and so prevent otherwise quite predictable problems.

   In addition to consulting breeders and breed books such as this one (which understandably have a positive breed bias), seek out as many

Especially for puppies, the first few weeks at home are the most important and influential days in the dog's life.

pet owners with your breed as you can find. Good points are obvious. What you want to find out are the breed-specific problems, so you can nip them in the bud. In particular, you should talk to owners with adolescent dogs and make a list of all anticipated problems. Most important, test drive at least half a dozen adolescent and adult dogs of your breed yourself. An 8-week-old puppy is deceptively easy to handle, but she will acquire adult size, speed and strength in just four months, so you should learn now what to prepare for.

Puppy and pet dog training classes offer a convenient venue to locate pet owners and observe dogs in action. For a list of suitable trainers in your area, contact the Association of Pet Dog Trainers (see chapter 9). You may also begin your basic owner training by observing other owners in class. Watch as many classes and test drive as many dogs as possible. Select an upbeat, dog-friendly, people-friendly, fun-and-games, puppydog pet training class to learn the ropes. Also, watch training videos and read training books. You must find out what to do and how to do it *before* you have to do it.

PRINCIPLES OF TRAINING

Most people think training comprises teaching the dog to do things such as sit, speak and roll over, but even a 4-week-old pup knows how to do these things already. Instead, the first step in training involves teaching the dog human words for each dog behavior and activity and for each aspect of the dog's environment. That way you, the owner, can more easily participate in the dog's domestic education by directing her to perform specific actions appropriately, that is, at the right time, in the right place and so on. Training opens communication channels, enabling an educated dog to at least understand her owner's requests.

In addition to teaching a dog what we want her to do, it is also necessary to teach her why she should do what we ask. Indeed, 95 percent of training revolves around motivating the dog to want to do what we want. Dogs often understand what their owners want; they just don't see the point of doing it—especially when the owner's repetitively boring and seemingly senseless instructions are totally at odds with much more pressing and exciting doggy distractions. It is not so much the dog that is being stubborn or dominant; rather, it is the owner who has failed to acknowledge the dog's needs and feelings and to approach training from the dog's point of view.

The Meaning of Instructions

The secret to successful training is learning how to use training lures to predict or prompt specific behaviors—to coax the dog to do what you want when you want. Any highly valued object (such as a treat or toy) may be used as a lure, which the dog will follow with her eyes and nose. Moving the lure in specific ways entices the dog to move her nose, head and entire body in specific ways. In fact, by learning the art of manipulating various lures, it is possible to teach the dog to assume virtually any body position and perform any action. Once you have control over the expression of the dog's behaviors and can elicit any body position or behavior at will, you can easily teach the dog to perform on request.

Tell your dog what you want her to do, use a lure to entice her to respond correctly, then profusely praise and maybe reward her once she performs the desired action. For example, verbally request "Fido, sit!" while you move a squeaky toy upwards and backwards over the dog's muzzle (lure-movement and hand signal), smile knowingly as she looks up (to follow the lure) and sits down (as a result of canine anatomical engineering), then praise her to distraction ("Gooood Fido!").

Squeak the toy, offer a training treat and give your dog and yourself a pat on the back.

Being able to elicit desired responses over and over enables the owner to reward the dog over and over. Consequently, the dog begins to think training is fun. For example, the more the dog is rewarded for sitting, the more she enjoys sitting. Eventually the dog comes to realize that, whereas most sitting is appreciated, sitting immediately upon request usually prompts especially enthusiastic praise and a slew of high-level rewards. The dog begins to sit on cue much of the time, showing that

Make your training session fun! If it's not fun, you won't enjoy it and neither will your dog.

OWNING A PARTY ANIMAL

It's a fact: The more of the world your puppy is exposed to, the more comfortable she'll be in it. Once your puppy's had her shots, start taking her everywhere with you. Encourage friendly interaction with strangers, expose her to different environments (towns, fields, beaches) and most important, enroll her in a puppy class where she'll get to play with other puppies. These simple, fun, shared activities will develop your pup into a confident socialite; reliable around other people and dogs.

she is starting to grasp the meaning of the owner's verbal request and hand signal.

Why Comply?

Most dogs enjoy initial lure-reward training and are only too happy to comply with their owners' wishes. Unfortunately, repetitive drilling without appreciative feedback tends to diminish the dog's enthusiasm until she eventually fails to see the point of complying anymore. Moreover, as the dog approaches adolescence she becomes more easily distracted as she develops other interests. Lengthy sessions with repetitive exercises tend to bore and demotivate both parties. If it's not fun, the owner doesn't do it and neither does the dog.

Integrate training into your dog's life: The greater number of training sessions each day and the shorter they are, the more willingly compliant your dog will become. Make sure to have a short (just a few seconds) training interlude before every enjoyable canine activity. For example, ask your dog to sit to greet people, to sit before you throw her Frisbee and to sit for her supper. Really, sitting is no different from a canine "Please." Also, include numerous short training interludes during every enjoyable canine pastime, for example, when playing with the dog or when she is running in the park. In this fashion, doggy distractions may be effectively converted into rewards for training. Just as all games have rules, fun becomes training . . . and training becomes fun.

Eventually, rewards actually become unnecessary to continue motivating your dog. If trained with consideration and kindness, performing the desired behaviors will become self-rewarding and, in a sense, your dog will motivate herself. Just as it is not necessary to reward a human companion during an enjoyable walk in the park, or following a game of tennis, it is hardly necessary to reward our best friend—the dog—for walking by our side or while playing fetch. Human company during enjoyable activities is reward enough for most dogs.

Even though your dog has become self-motivating, it's still good to praise and pet her a lot and offer rewards once in a while, especially for a job well done. And if for no other reason, praising and rewarding others is good for the human heart.

73

TRAINER'S TOOLS

Most effective training tools are not found in stores; they come from within ourselves. In addition to a willing dog, all you really need is a functional human brain, gentle hands, a loving heart and a good attitude.

In terms of equipment, all dogs do require a quality buckle collar to sport dog tags and to attach the leash (for safety and to comply with local leash laws). Hollow chew toys (like Kongs or sterilized longbones) and a dog bed or collapsible crate are musts for housetraining. Three additional tools are required:

1. specific lures (training treats and toys) to predict and prompt specific desired behaviors;

2. rewards (praise, affection, training treats and toys) to reinforce for the dog what a lot of fun it all is; and

3. knowledge—how to convert the dog's favorite activities and games (potential distractions to training) into "life-rewards," which may be employed to facilitate training.

The most powerful of these is knowledge. Education is the key! Watch training classes, participate in training classes, watch videos, read

You don't have to wait for your dog to do something spectacular to reward her. Rewarding your Shih Tzu for simply sitting quietly with her toys will teach her the way in which you want her to behave.

FINDING A TRAINER

Have fun with your dog, take a training class! But don't just sign on any dotted line, find a trainer whose approach and style you like and whose students (and their dogs) are really learning. Ask to visit a class to observe a trainer in action. For the names of trainers near you, ask your veterinarian, your pet supply store, your dog-owning neighbors or call (800) PET-DOGS (the Association of Pet Dog Trainers).

books, enjoy play-training with your dog and then your dog will say "Please," and your dog will say "Thank you!"

HOUSETRAINING

If dogs were left to their own devices, certainly they would chew, dig and bark for entertainment and then no doubt highlight a few areas of their living space with sprinkles of urine, in much the same way we decorate by hanging pictures. Consequently, when we ask a dog to live with us, we must teach her *where* she may dig, *where* she may perform her toilet duties, *what* she may chew and *when* she may bark. After all, when left at

home alone for many hours, we cannot expect the dog to amuse herself by completing crosswords or watching TV!

Also, it would be decidedly unfair to keep the house rules a secret from the dog, and then get angry and punish the poor critter for inevitably transgressing rules she did not even know existed. Remember: Without adequate education and guidance, the dog will be forced to establish her own rules—doggy rules—and most probably will be at odds with the owner's view of domestic living.

Since most problems develop during the first few days the dog is at home, prospective dog owners must be certain they are quite clear about the principles of housetraining *before* they get a dog. Early misbehaviors quickly become established as the *status quo*—becoming firmly entrenched as hard-to-break bad habits, which set the precedent for years to come. Make sure to teach your dog good habits right from the start. Good habits are just as hard to break as bad ones!

Ideally, when a new dog comes home, try to arrange for someone to be present as much as possible during the first few days (for adult dogs) or weeks for puppies. With only a little forethought, it is surprisingly easy to find a puppy sitter, such as a retired person, who would be willing to eat from your refrigerator and watch your television while keeping an eye on the newcomer to encourage the dog to play with chew toys and to ensure she goes outside on a regular basis.

Potty Training

Follow these steps to teach the dog where she should relieve herself:

1. never let her make a single mistake;

2. let her know where you want her to go; and

3. handsomely reward her for doing so: "GOOOOOOOD DOG!!!" liver treat, liver treat, liver treat!

Preventing Mistakes

A single mistake is a training disaster, since it heralds many more in future weeks. And each time the dog soils the house, this further reinforces the dog's unfortunate preference for an indoor, carpeted toilet. Do not let an unhousetrained dog have full run of the house.

When you are away from home, or cannot pay full attention, confine the dog to an area where elimination is appropriate, such as an outdoor run or, better still, a small, comfortable indoor kennel with access to an outdoor run. When confined in this manner, most dogs will naturally housetrain themselves.

If that's not possible, confine the dog to an area, such as a utility room, kitchen, basement or garage, where elimination may not be desired in the long run but as an interim measure it is certainly preferable to doing it all around the house. Use

HOUSETRAINING 1-2-3

1. Prevent Mistakes. When you can't supervise your puppy, confine her in a single room or in her crate (but don't leave her for too long!). Puppy-proof the area by laying down newspapers so that if she does make a mistake, it won't matter.

2. Teach Where. Take your puppy to the spot you want her to use every hour.

3. When she goes, praise her profusely and give her three favorite treats.

newspaper to cover the floor of the dog's day room. The newspaper may be used to soak up the urine and to wrap up and dispose of the feces. Once your dog develops a preferred spot for eliminating, it is only necessary to cover that part of the floor with newspaper. The smaller papered area may then be moved (only a little each day) towards the door to the outside. Thus the dog will develop the tendency to go to the door when she needs to relieve herself.

Never confine an unhousetrained dog to a crate for long periods. Doing so would force the dog to soil the crate and ruin its usefulness as an aid for housetraining (see the following discussion).

Teaching Where

In order to teach your dog where you would like her to do her business, you have to be there to direct the proceedings—an obvious, yet often neglected, fact of life. In order to be there to teach the dog where to go, you need to know *when* she needs to go. Indeed, the success of housetraining depends on the owner's ability to predict these times. Certainly, a regular feeding schedule will facilitate prediction somewhat, but there is

nothing like "loading the deck" and influencing the timing of the outcome yourself!

Whenever you are at home, make sure the dog is under constant supervision and/or confined to a small area. If already well trained, simply instruct the dog to lie down in her bed or basket. Alternatively, confine the dog to a crate (doggy den) or tie-down (a short, 18-inch lead that can be clipped to an eye hook in the baseboard near her bed). Short-term close confinement strongly inhibits urination and defecation, since the dog does not want to soil her sleeping area. Thus, when you release the puppydog each hour, she will definitely need to urinate immediately and defecate every third or fourth hour. Keep the dog confined to her doggy den and take her to her intended toilet area each hour, every hour and on the hour. When taking your dog outside, instruct her to sit quietly before opening the door— she will soon learn to sit by the door when she needs to go out!

Teaching Why

Being able to predict when the dog needs to go enables the owner to be on the spot to praise and reward the dog. Each hour, hurry the dog to the intended toilet area in the yard, issue the appropriate instruction ("Go pee!" or "Go poop!"), then give the dog three to four minutes to produce. Praise and offer a couple of training treats when successful. The treats are important because many people fail to praise their dogs with feeling—and housetraining is hardly the time for understatement. So either loosen up and enthusiastically praise that dog: "Wuzzzer-wuzzer-wuzzer, hoooser good wuffer den? Hoooo went pee for Daddy?" Or say "Good dog!" as best you can and offer the treats for effect.

Following elimination is an ideal time for a spot of play-training in the yard or house. Also, an empty dog may be allowed greater freedom around the house for the next half hour or so, just as long as you keep an eye out to make sure she does not get into other kinds of mischief. If you are preoccupied and cannot pay full attention, confine the dog to her doggy den once more to enjoy a peaceful snooze or to play with her many chew toys.

If your dog does not eliminate within the allotted time outside—no biggie! Back to her doggy den, and then try again after another hour.

As I own large dogs, I always feel more relaxed walking an empty dog, knowing that I will not need to finish our stroll weighted down with bags of feces!

Beware of falling into the trap of walking the dog to get her to eliminate. The good ol' dog walk is such an enormous highlight in the dog's life that it represents the single biggest potential reward in domestic dogdom. However, when in a hurry, or during inclement weather, many owners abruptly terminate the walk the moment the dog has done her business. This, in effect, severely punishes the dog for doing the right thing, in the right place at the right time. Consequently, many dogs become strongly inhibited from eliminating outdoors because they know it will signal an abrupt end to an otherwise thoroughly enjoyable walk.

Instead, instruct the dog to relieve herself in the yard prior to going for a walk. If you follow the above instructions, most dogs soon learn to eliminate on cue. As soon as the dog eliminates, praise (and offer a treat or two)—"Good dog! Let's go walkies!" Use the walk as a reward for eliminating in the yard. If the dog does not go, put her back in her doggy den and think about a

Short-term close confinement teaches the dog that occasional quiet moments are a reality of domestic living.

walk later on. You will find with a "No feces—no walk" policy, your dog will become one of the fastest defecators in the business.

TOYS THAT EARN THEIR KEEP

To entertain even the most distracted of dogs, while you're home or away, have a selection of the following toys on hand: hollow chew toys (like Kongs, sterilized hollow longbones and cubes or balls that can be stuffed with kibble). Smear peanut butter or honey on the inside of the hollow toy or bone and stuff the bone with kibble and your dog will think of nothing else but working the object to get at the food. Great to take your dog's mind off the fact that you've left the house.

If you do not have a backyard, instruct the dog to eliminate right outside your front door prior to the walk. Not only will this facilitate clean up and disposal of the feces in your own trash can but, also, the walk may again be used as a colossal reward.

CHEWING AND BARKING

Your puppydog is extremely impressionable during her first few weeks at home. Regular confinement at this time soon exerts a calming influence over the dog's personality. Remember, once the dog is housetrained and calmer, there will be a whole lifetime ahead for the dog to enjoy full run of the house and garden. On the other hand, by letting the newcomer have unrestricted access to the entire household and allowing her to run willy-nilly, she will most certainly develop a bunch of behavior problems in short order, no doubt necessitating confinement later in life. It would not be fair to remedially restrain and confine a dog you have trained, through neglect, to run free.

When confining the dog, make sure she always has an impressive array of suitable chew toys. Kongs and sterilized longbones (both readily available from pet stores) make the best chew toys, since they are hollow and may be stuffed with treats to heighten the dog's interest. For example, by stuffing the little hole at the top of a Kong with a small piece of freeze-dried liver, the dog will not want to leave it alone.

Remember, treats do not have to be junk food and they certainly should not represent extra calories.

If stuffed chew toys are reserved especially for times the dog is confined, the puppydog will soon learn to enjoy quiet moments in her doggy den and she will quickly develop a chew-toy habit—a good habit! This is a simple autoshaping process; all the owner has to do is set up the situation and the dog all but trains herself—easy and effective. Even when the dog is given run of the house, her first inclination will be to indulge her rewarding chew-toy habit rather than destroy less-attractive household articles, such as curtains, carpets, chairs and compact disks. Similarly, a chew-toy chewer will be less inclined to scratch and chew herself excessively. Also, if the dog busies herself as a recreational chewer, she will be less inclined to develop into a recreational barker or digger when left at home alone.

COME AND SIT

Most puppies will happily approach virtually anyone, whether called or not; that is, until they collide with adolescence and develop other more important doggy interests, such as sniffing a multiplicity of exquisite odors on the grass. Your mission, Mr./Ms. Owner, is to teach and reward the pup for coming reliably, willingly and happily when called— and you have just three months to get it done. Unless adequately reinforced, your puppy's tendency to approach people will self-destruct by adolescence.

Call your dog ("Fido, come!"), open your arms (and maybe squat down) as a welcoming signal, waggle a treat or toy as a lure and reward the puppydog when she comes running. Do not wait to praise the dog until she reaches you—she may come 95 percent of the way and then run off after some distraction. Instead, praise the dog's first step towards you and continue praising enthusiastically for every step she takes in your direction.

When the rapidly approaching puppy dog is three lengths away from impact, instruct her to sit ("Fido, sit!") and hold the lure in front of you in an outstretched hand to prevent her from hitting you mid-chest and knocking you flat on your back! As Fido decelerates to nose the lure, move the treat upwards and backwards just over her muzzle with an upwards motion of your extended arm (palm-upwards). As the dog looks up to follow the lure, she will sit down (if she jumps up, you are holding the lure too high). Praise the dog for sitting. Move backwards and call her again. Repeat this many times over, always praising when Fido comes and sits; on occasion, reward her.

For the first couple of trials, use a training treat both as a lure to entice the dog to come and sit and as a reward for doing so. Thereafter, try to use different items as lures and rewards. For example, lure the dog with a Kong or Frisbee but reward her with a food treat. Or lure the dog with a food treat but pat her and throw a tennis ball as a reward. After just a few repetitions, dispense with the lures and rewards; the dog will begin to respond willingly to your verbal requests and hand signals just for the prospect of praise from your heart and affection from your hands.

Even though your dog quickly masters obedient recalls in the house, her reliability may falter when playing in the backyard or local park. Ironically, it is the owner who has unintentionally trained the dog not to respond in these instances. By allowing the dog to play and run around and otherwise have a good time, but then to call the dog to put her on leash to take her home, the dog quickly learns playing is fun but training is a drag. Thus, playing in the park becomes a severe distraction, which works against training. Bad news!

Instead, whether playing with the dog off leash or on leash, request

No matter what you are training your Shih Tzu to do, remember to praise her profusely for a job well done.

80

her to come at frequent intervals—say, every minute or so. On most occasions, praise and pet the dog for a few seconds while she is sitting, then tell her to go play again. For especially fast recalls, offer a couple of training treats and take the time to praise and pet the dog enthusiastically before releasing her. The dog will learn that coming when called is not necessarily the end of the play session, and neither is it the end of the world; rather, it signals an enjoyable, quality time-out with the owner before resuming play once more. In fact, playing in the park now becomes a very effective life-reward, which works to facilitate training by reinforcing each obedient and timely recall. Good news!

SIT, DOWN, STAND AND ROLLOVER

Teaching the dog a variety of body positions is easy for owner and dog, impressive for spectators and extremely useful for all. Using lure-reward techniques, it is possible to train several positions at once to verbal commands or hand signals (which impress the socks off onlookers).

Sit and down—the two control commands—prevent or resolve nearly a hundred behavior problems. For example, if the dog happily and obediently sits or lies down when requested, she cannot jump on visitors, dash out the front door, run around and chase her tail, pester other dogs, harass cats or annoy family, friends or strangers. Additionally, "Sit" or "Down" are the best emergency commands for off-leash control.

It is easier to teach and maintain a reliable sit than maintain a reliable recall. Sit is the purest and simplest of commands—either the dog is sitting or she is not. If there is any change of circumstances or potential danger in the park, for example, simply instruct the dog to sit. If she sits, you have a number of options: Allow the dog to resume playing when she is safe, walk up and put the dog on leash or call the dog. The dog will be much more likely to come when called if she has already acknowledged her compliance by sitting. If the dog does not sit in the park—train her to!

Stand and rollover-stay are the two positions for examining the dog. Your veterinarian will love you to distraction if you take a little time to teach the dog to stand still and roll over and play possum. Also, your vet bills will be smaller because it will take the veterinarian less time to examine your dog. The rollover-stay is an especially useful command and is really just a variation of the down-stay: Whereas the dog lies prone in the traditional down, she lies supine in the rollover-stay.

As with teaching come and sit, the training techniques to teach the dog to assume all other body positions on cue are user-friendly and dog-friendly. Simply give the appropriate request, lure the dog into the desired body position using a training treat or toy and then praise (and maybe reward) the dog as soon as she complies. Try not to touch the dog to get her to respond. If you teach the dog by guiding her into position, the dog will quickly learn that rump-pressure means sit, for example, but as yet you still have no control over your dog if she is just 6 feet away. It will still be necessary to teach the dog to sit on request. So do not make training a time-consuming two-step process; instead, teach the dog to sit to a verbal request or hand signal from the outset. Once the dog sits willingly when requested, by all means use your hands to pet the dog when she does so.

To teach down when the dog is already sitting, say "Fido, down!", hold the lure in one hand (palm down) and lower that hand to the floor between the dog's forepaws. As the dog lowers her head to follow the lure, slowly move the lure away from the dog just a fraction (in front of her paws). The dog will lie down as she stretches her nose forward to follow the lure. Praise the dog when she does so. If the dog stands up, you pulled the lure away too far and too quickly.

When teaching the dog to lie down from the standing position, say "Down" and lower the lure to the floor as before. Once the dog has lowered her forequarters and assumed a play bow, gently and slowly move the lure towards the dog between her forelegs. Praise the dog as soon as her rear end plops down.

After just a couple of trials it will be possible to alternate sits and downs and have the dog energetically perform doggy push-ups. Praise the dog a lot, and after half a dozen or so push-ups reward the dog with a training treat or toy. You will notice the more energetically you move your arm—upwards (palm up) to get the dog to sit, and downwards (palm down) to get the dog to lie down—the more energetically the dog responds to your requests. Now try training the dog in silence and you will notice she has also learned to respond to hand signals. Yeah! Not too shabby for the first session.

To teach stand from the sitting position, say "Fido, stand," slowly move the lure half a dog-length away from the dog's nose, keeping it at nose level, and praise the dog as she stands to follow the lure. As soon as the dog stands, lower the lure to just beneath the dog's chin to entice her to look down; otherwise she will stand and then sit immediately. To prompt the dog to stand from the down position, move the lure half a dog-length upwards and away from the dog, holding the lure at standing nose height from the floor.

Teaching rollover is best started from the down position, with the dog lying on one side, or at least with both hind legs stretched out on the same side. Say "Fido, bang!" and move the lure backwards and alongside the dog's muzzle to her elbow (on the side of her outstretched hind legs). Once the dog looks to the side and backwards, very slowly move the lure upwards to the dog's shoulder and backbone. Tickling the dog in the goolies (groin area) often invokes

a reflex-raising of the hind leg as an appeasement gesture, which facilitates the tendency to roll over. If you move the lure too quickly and the dog jumps into the standing position, have patience and start again. As soon as the dog rolls onto her back, keep the lure stationary and mezmerize the dog with a relaxing tummy rub.

To teach rollover-stay when the dog is standing or moving, say "Fido, bang!" and give the appropriate hand signal (with index finger pointed and thumb cocked in true Sam Spade fashion), then in one fluid movement lure her to first lie down and then rollover-stay as above.

Teaching the dog to stay in each of the above four positions becomes a piece of cake after first teaching the dog not to worry at the toy or treat training lure. This is best accomplished by hand feeding dinner kibble. Hold a piece of kibble firmly in your hand and softly instruct "Off!" Ignore any licking and slobbering for however long the dog worries at the treat, but say "Take it!" and offer the kibble the instant the dog breaks contact with her muzzle. Repeat this a few times, and then up the ante and insist the dog remove her muzzle for one whole second before offering the kibble. Then progressively refine your criteria and have the dog not touch your hand (or treat) for longer and longer periods on each trial, such as for two seconds, four seconds, then six, ten, fifteen, twenty, thirty seconds and so on.

The dog soon learns: (1) worrying at the treat never gets results, whereas (2) noncontact is often rewarded after a variable time lapse.

Teaching "Off!" has many useful applications in its own right. Additionally, instructing the dog not to touch a training lure often produces spontaneous and magical stays. Request the dog to stand-stay, for example, and not to touch the lure. At first set your sights on a short two-second stay before rewarding the dog. (Remember, every long journey begins with a single step.) However, on subsequent trials, gradually and progressively increase the length of stay required to receive a reward. In no time at all your dog will stand calmly for a minute or so.

RELEVANCY TRAINING

Once you have taught the dog what you expect her to do when requested to come, sit, lie down, stand, rollover and stay, the time is right to teach the dog why she should comply with

your wishes. The secret is to have many (many) extremely short training interludes (two to five seconds each) at numerous (numerous) times during the course of the dog's day. Especially work with the dog immediately before the dog's good times and during the dog's good times. For example, ask your dog to sit and/or lie down each time before opening doors, serving meals, offering treats and tummy rubs; ask the dog to perform a few controlled doggy push-ups before letting her off leash or throwing a tennis ball; and perhaps request the dog to sit-down-sit-stand-down-stand-rollover before inviting her to cuddle on the couch.

Similarly, request the dog to sit many times during play or on walks, and in no time at all the dog will be only too pleased to follow your instructions because she has learned that a compliant response heralds all sorts of goodies. Basically all you are trying to teach the dog is how to say please: "Please throw the tennis ball. Please may I snuggle on the couch."

Remember, it is important to keep training interludes short and to have many short sessions each and every day. The shortest (and most useful) session comprises asking the dog to sit and then go play during a play session. When trained this way, your dog will soon associate training with good times. In fact, the dog may be unable to distinguish between training and good times and, indeed, there should be no distinction. The warped concept that training involves forcing the dog to comply and/or dominating her will is totally at odds with the picture of a truly well-trained dog. In reality, enjoying a game of training with a dog is no different from enjoying a game of backgammon or tennis with a friend; and walking with a dog should be no different from strolling with a spouse, or with buddies on the golf course.

WALK BY YOUR SIDE

Many people attempt to teach a dog to heel by putting her on a leash and physically correcting the dog when she makes mistakes. There are a number of things seriously wrong with this approach, the first being that most people do not want precision heeling; rather, they simply want the dog to follow or walk by their side. Second, when physically restrained during "training," even

This owner chooses to stay indoors when practicing with her puppy on leash.

though the dog may grudgingly mope by your side when "handcuffed" on leash, let's see what happens when she is off leash. History! The dog is in the next county because she never enjoyed walking with you on leash and you have no control over her off leash. So let's just teach the dog off leash from the outset to want to walk with us. Third, if the dog has not been trained to heel, it is a trifle hasty to think about punishing the poor dog for making mistakes and breaking heeling rules she didn't even know existed. This is simply not fair! Surely, if the dog had been adequately taught how to heel, she would seldom make mistakes and hence there would be no need to correct the dog.

Let's teach the dog to enjoy following us and to want to walk by our side off leash. Before going on outdoor walks, it is necessary to teach the dog not to pull. Then it becomes easy to teach on-leash walking and heeling because the dog already wants to walk with you, she is familiar with the desired walking and heeling positions and she knows not to pull.

This Shih Tzu has been taught to not pull on leash and to walk calmly by her owner's side.

FOLLOWING

Start by training your dog to follow you. Many puppies will follow if you simply walk away from them and maybe click your fingers or chuckle. Adult dogs may require additional enticement to stimulate them to follow, such as a training lure or, at the very least, a lively trainer. To teach the dog to follow: (1) keep walking and (2) walk away from the dog. If the dog attempts to lead or lag, change pace; slow down if the dog forges too far ahead, but speed up if she lags too far behind. Say "Steady!" or "Easy!" each time before you slow down and "Quickly!" or "Hustle!" each time before you speed up, and the dog will learn to change pace on cue. If the dog lags or leads too far, or if she wanders right or left, simply walk quickly in the opposite direction and maybe even run away from the dog and hide.

Remember, following has a lot to do with attitude—your attitude! Most probably your dog will not want to follow Mr. Grumpy Troll with the personality of wilted lettuce. Lighten up—walk with a jaunty step, whistle a happy tune, sing, skip and tell jokes to your dog and she will be right there by your side.

CHAPTER NINE

Resources

BOOKS

About Shih Tzu

Cuncliffe, Juliette. *The Complete Shih Tzu.* Cincinnati: Seven Hills Book Distributors, 1993.

Joris, Victor. *The Complete Shih Tzu.* New York: Howell Book House, 1994.

White, Jo Ann. *Official Book of the Shih Tzu.* Neptune, NJ: Tfh., 1998.

About Health Care

American Kennel Club. *American Kennel Club Dog Care and Training.* New York: Howell Book House, 1991.

Carlson, Delbert, DVM, and James Giffen, MD. *Dog Owner's Home Veterinary Handbook.* New York: Howell Book House, 1992.

DeBitetto, James, DVM, and Sarah Hodgson. *You & Your Puppy.* New York: Howell Book House, 1995.

Lane, Marion. *The Humane Society of the United States Complete Guide to Dog Care.* New York: Little, Brown & Co., 1998.

McGinnis, Terri. *The Well Dog Book.* New York: Random House, 1991.

Schwartz, Stephanie, DVM. *First Aid for Dogs: An Owner's Guide to a Happy Healthy Pet.* New York: Howell Book House, 1998.

Volhard, Wendy and Kerry L. Brown. *The Holistic Guide for a Healthy Dog.* New York: Howell Book House, 1995.

About Training

Ammen, Amy. *Training in No Time.* New York: Howell Book House, 1995.

Benjamin, Carol Lea. *Mother Knows Best.* New York: Howell Book House, 1985.

Bohnenkamp, Gwen. *Manners for the Modern Dog.* San Francisco: Perfect Paws, 1990.

Dunbar, Ian, Ph.D., MRCVS. *Dr. Dunbar's Good Little Book.* James & Kenneth Publishers, 2140 Shattuck Ave. #2406, Berkeley, CA 94704. (510) 658-8588. Order from Publisher.

Evans, Job Michael. *People, Pooches and Problems.* New York: Howell Book House, 1991.

Palika, Liz. *All Dogs Need Some Training.* New York: Howell Book House, 1997.

Volhard, Jack and Melissa Bartlett. *What All Good Dogs Should Know: The Sensible Way to Train.* New York: Howell Book House, 1991.

About Activities

Hall, Lynn. *Dog Showing for Beginners.* New York: Howell Book House, 1994.

O'Neil, Jackie. *All About Agility.* New York: Howell Book House, 1998.

Simmons-Moake, Jane. *Agility Training, The Fun Sport for All Dogs.* New York: Howell Book House, 1991.

Vanacore, Connie. *Dog Showing: An Owner's Guide.* New York: Howell Book House, 1990.

Volhard, Jack and Wendy. *The Canine Good Citizen.* New York: Howell Book House, 1994.

MAGAZINES

THE AKC GAZETTE, The Official Journal for the Sport of Purebred Dogs
American Kennel Club
260 Madison Ave.
New York, NY 10016
www.akc.org

DOG FANCY
Fancy Publications
3 Burroughs
Irvine, CA 92618
(714) 855-8822
http://dogfancy.com

DOG & KENNEL
7-L Dundas Circle
Greensboro, NC 27407
(336) 292-4047
www.dogandkennel.com

DOG WORLD
Maclean Hunter Publishing Corp.
500 N. Dearborn, Ste. 1100
Chicago, IL 60610
(312) 396-0600
www.dogworldmag.com

PETLIFE: Your Companion Animal Magazine
Magnolia Media Group
1400 Two Tandy Center
Fort Worth, TX 76102
(800) 767-9377
www.petlifeweb.com

MORE INFORMATION ABOUT SHIH TZU

National Breed Club

AMERICAN SHIH TZU CLUB, INC.
Corresponding Secretary:

Bonnie Prato
5252 Shafter Avenue
Oakland, CA 94618

Breeder Contact:

Mrs. Andy Hicock Warner
23 Big Oak Road
Dillsburg, PA 17019
(717) 432-4351

Breed Rescue:

Phyllis Celmer
(760) 942-0874

The Club can send you information on all aspects of the breed including the names and addresses of breed clubs in your area, as well as obedience clubs. Inquire about membership.

The American Kennel Club

The American Kennel Club (AKC), devoted to the advancement of purebred dogs, is the oldest and largest registry organization in this country. Every breed recognized by the AKC has a national (parent) club. National clubs are a great source of information on your breed. The affiliated clubs hold AKC events and use AKC rules to hold performance events, dog shows, educational programs, health clinics and training classes. The AKC staff is divided between offices in New York City and Raleigh, North Carolina. The AKC has an excellent Web site that provides information on the organization and all AKC-recognized breeds. The address is **www.akc.org**.

For registration and performance events information, or for customer service, contact:

THE AMERICAN KENNEL CLUB
5580 Centerview Dr., Suite 200
Raleigh, NC 27606
(919) 233-9767

The AKC's executive offices and the AKC Library (open to the public) are at this address:

THE AMERICAN KENNEL CLUB
260 Madison Ave.
New York, New York 10016
(212) 696-8200 (general information)
(212) 696-8246 (AKC Library)
www.akc.org

UNITED KENNEL CLUB
100 E. Kilgore Rd.
Kalamazoo, MI 49001-5598
(616) 343-9020
www.ukcdogs.com

AMERICAN RARE BREED ASSOCIATION
9921 Frank Tippett Rd.
Cheltenham, MD 20623
(301) 868-5718 (voice or fax)
www.arba.org

CANADIAN KENNEL CLUB
89 Skyway Ave., Ste. 100
Etobicoke, Ontario
Canada M9W 6R4
(416) 675-5511
www.ckc.ca

ORTHOPEDIC FOUNDATION FOR ANIMALS (OFA)
2300 E. Nifong Blvd.
Columbia, MO 65201-3856
(314) 442-0418
www.offa.org/

Trainers

Animal Behavior & Training Associates (ABTA)
9018 Balboa Blvd., Ste. 591
Northridge, CA 91325
(800) 795-3294
www.Good-dawg.com

Association of Pet Dog Trainers (APDT)
(800) PET-DOGS
www.apdt.com

National Association of Dog Obedience
Instructors (NADOI)
729 Grapevine Highway, Ste. 369
Hurst, TX 76054-2085
www.kimberly.uidaho.edu/nadoi

Associations

Delta Society
P.O. Box 1080
Renton, WA 98507-1080

(Promotes the human/animal bond
through pet-assisted therapy and other
programs)
www.petsforum.com/DELTASOCIETY/
dsi400.htm

Dog Writers Association of America
(DWAA)
Sally Cooper, Secretary
222 Woodchuck Lane
Harwinton, CT 06791
www.dwaa.org

National Association for Search and
Rescue (NASAR)
4500 Southgate Place, Ste. 100
Chantilly, VA 20157
(703) 222-6277
www.nasar.org

Therapy Dogs International
6 Hilltop Rd.
Mendham, NJ 07945

OTHER USEFUL RESOURCES— WEB SITES

General Information— Links to Additional Sites, On-Line Shopping

www.k9web.com – resources for the dog
world
www.netpet.com – pet related products,
software and services
www.apapets.com – The American Pet
Association
www.dogandcatbooks.com – book catalog
www.dogbooks.com – on-line bookshop
www.animal.discovery.com/ – cable
television channel on-line

Health

www.avma.org – American Veterinary
Medical Association (AVMA)

www.aplb.org – Association for Pet Loss
Bereavement (APLB)—contains an
index of national hot lines for on-line
and office counseling.

www.netfopets.com/AskTheExperts.
html – veterinary questions answered
on-line.

Breed Information

www.bestdogs.com/news/ – newsgroup
www.cheta.net/connect/canine/breeds/ –
Canine Connections Breed
Information Index

Put a picture of your dog
in this box

Your Dog's Name _____

Your Dog's License Number _____

Date of Birth _____

Your Dog's Veterinarian _____

Address _____

Phone Number _____

Medications _____

Vet Emergency Number _____

Additional Emergency Numbers _____

Feeding Instructions _____

Exercise Routine _____

Favorite Treats _____

Muzzle

Stop

Skull

Shoulder

Crest

Neck

Withers

Back

Stifle or Knee

Hock

Toes